*WILDLIFE BEGINS AT HOME*

# WILDLIFE BEGINS AT HOME

TONY SOPER

Illustrations by Robert Gillmor

DAVID & CHARLES
NEWTON ABBOT LONDON
NORTH POMFRET (VT) VANCOUVER

By the same author:
The Shell Book of Beachcombing
The New Bird Table Book
The Wreck of the Torrey Canyon
(with Crispin Gill and Frank Booker)
Penguins (with John Sparks)
Owls (with John Sparks)


For Hilary


ISBN 0 7153 7111 8
Library of Congress Catalog Card Number 75-10700

Set in 12 on 13 Bembo and printed in Great Britain
by Redwood Burn Limited Trowbridge
for David & Charles (Publishers) Limited
South Devon House    Newton Abbot    Devon

Published in the United States of America
for David & Charles Inc
North Pomfret    Vermont 05053    USA

Published in Canada by Douglas David &
Charles Limited    132 Philip Avenue
North Vancouver BC

# CONTENTS

# ILLUSTRATIONS

Nay, gather not that Filbert, Nicholas,
There is a maggot there . . . it is his house . . .

'The Filbert' Robert Southey (1774–1843)

# 1 WILD NEIGHBOURS

Not so very long ago, three thousand years or so, Neolithic man first got the feel of an axe in his hand. And the face of Britain got a rude shock. Until then man had acted out his role as a hunter and a gatherer of fruits and nuts and such vegetation as pleased him, but with that axe he wielded a terrible power, cutting down the broad-leafed woodland that had flourished since the Ice Age. Slashing and burning, he cleared land to grow cereals and grass, to bake bread and nourish domesticated cattle and sheep. Man the hunter became man the farmer and gardener, dominating the landscape and doing it his way.

So the Britain which was once an enormous forest is now a cultivated land of cities and grass and arable farms. But a modest ten per cent of the woodland remains, to give us pleasure and interest out of all proportion to its size. The wild creatures of the forest, by and large, are the ones that share our houses and gardens today and in seeking to enjoy and learn something about our wild neighbours it is well to remember that, from their point of view, our gardens are simply slices of woodland edge. Some species, as we shall see, are more inclined to think of our houses as coastal cliffs and caves, but they are in the minority.

One thing is certain. Whether you like it or not, you will have wild animals and wild plants joining you to live in, on and around what you may fondly regard as 'your' castle. Try as you may, cover the plot with concrete even, you will still be host to green algae, lichens and fungi. Even the tidiest, most manicured garden, will provide plant food. And where there are plants there will be bugs to graze them, and birds to eat the bugs. You will have a hard job to avoid the companionship of

Chaffinch

sparrows and starlings! I hope you are prepared to offer a cautious welcome to these uninvited guests, for they will repay your interest many times over.

The pleasures are real. First in identifying the visitor, then in watching the way it behaves and adapts to the homestead life, and seeing the manner of its comings and goings and relationships with other visitors. It is not necessary to travel to remote places in order to enjoy nature. A healthy slice of it lies on the other side of your garden window, and a not inconsiderable slice actually lives in the house with you!

A town house, with a garden of windowboxes, a paved yard or a roof area, may only attract a few flying insects and visiting house sparrows and pigeons. A small plot with a few bushes and trees will see an influx of blackbirds and a few tits. A larger garden with more trees, more shrubbery and a lawn will see robins and dunnocks, chaffinches, greenfinches, wrens and perhaps a hedgehog. With mature trees the woodland species come flooding in – jays, wood pigeons, more finches, treecreepers, blackcaps and thrushes, squirrels and owls. A mature garden is good news for a whole host of bugs, birds and beasts.

A newly constructed house with a lot of bare earth and newly planted saplings offers little attraction, so at this stage a well-stocked birdtable and a drinking/bathing pool are important. Natural food will be scarce so make special provision. The species you see will at first depend on the kind of country which has been converted. If your house was built on a drained saltmarsh then you may find meadow pipits coming to feed on the birdtable, as happened to John Burton, a friend of mine living near Bristol. Mostly, though, the ecological changes wrought by the builder result in the less adaptable species disappearing, trying their luck elsewhere. New building will be very bad news for specialist and finicky creatures like stone curlews, wheatears, dartford warblers, bearded tits and snipe – all animals which require open space and don't take kindly to disruption of their hunting lands.

But while heath and marshland species are ill served, gardens are an acceptable substitute for woodland and some aquatic species. When ecological succession – and a certain amount of management – provides mature trees, some decaying timber, creeper-clad walls and an abundance of shrubbery and secret places, then the animal population will show a distinct improvement. Plenty of light, plenty of shady corners, trees, shrubs and grassy glades. Plenty of natural food and shelter. Birdtable scraps and gadgets. A grassy lawn and a pond. All this adds up to good news for birds and for mammals like squirrels, foxes, hedgehogs and moles. Small birds are happy and flourish and, if you have a decent-sized lawn, you'll also find magpies, rooks, jackdaws, gulls, starlings and pigeons.

*To build, to plant, whatever you intend,*
*To rear the column, or the arch to bend,*
*To swell the terrace, or to sink the grot;*
*In all, let nature never be forgot.*

'*Epistle to Richard Boyle, Earl of Burlington*' Alexander Pope

The boundary to your property is an important consideration, and the character of the country on the other side of it is crucial. If you are lucky enough to have a long-established hedge-bank you have a trump card, for it will be a home base for a regiment of exciting creatures. But brick or stone walls, especially if they offer nooks and crannies, or even posts and rails, will develop a community of their own. And if you are neighbours with a park or churchyard, railway embankment or allotments, these extend the potential foraging range for animals.

In your own patch you must regard yourself as the dominant animal. It may not be exclusively your own castle, for other creatures share it whether you like it or not, but you wield a great deal of power. It may be easy to think that by controlling one small patch, providing a few pretty flowers and attracting a few pretty blue tits, you are not of much significance to planet earth, but that is decidedly not the case. The oxygen balance of the world is affected by the trees you plant. (And even if you have no garden at all you can do your stuff by making your roof into a green place with grass and plants). The character of your garden, whether it is bare earth or grass or green plants, will affect the amount of solar radiation which is reflected back from the earth. Everything matters, and a biologically healthy and productive garden has fundamental significance.

In our relationships to our home base we reflect many different attitudes. The Japanese garden was inspired by the idea of man as a fully integrated part of nature. The Renaissance garden, inspired by the conceit of man as master of nature, was a disastrous concept. Indeed a garden will offer many clues to the cultural attitudes of the period in which it was designed.

Gardens have many functions. There are vegetable-producing kitchen gardens, market gardens and herb gardens. But the garden we are interested in here is the area of land associated with a dwelling

Hedgehogs are at home in mature gardens where they hunt slugs and other juicy morsels (*Pat Morris*)

house, in effect an extension of that house, called upon to provide some food, much pleasure and a place to hang the washing. Over the years it has been 'civilised' with changing fashions ushering in the patio, the fountain and the swimming pool. Fountains and swimming pools are pretty bad news for animals, the one simply confusing a good hunting pond and the other negatively sterile.

Neolithic man had plenty of room, so he could afford the wasteful techniques of slashing down trees, burning a clearing and moving on after a season or two of cereal crops. But his type of gardening is hardly feasible for those of us with our hands on a very small, but permanent acreage. Left to itself, our patch would slowly revert to primeval forest. To maintain a moderately stable and attractive (to us) environment we have to work at it, though by planning carefully we can promote a garden which largely looks after itself. The principles involved are simple enough. Bare soil is an abomination which nature abhors, and to maintain it will involve a never-ending fight against 'weeds'. In a vegetable patch you have an example of primary production – cabbages from bare earth – and to maintain that production will involve constant effort, importing new nutrients to replace those 'lost' when you eat the cabbage, and replanting new seed and eliminating unwanted growth. This kind of thing is acceptable when the object is to produce food to sustain ourselves, but as a continuing technique it is madness in a pleasure garden, tolerable only if you actually enjoy endless work! By contrast with that vegetable patch, a mature scrubby corner of the garden may be less productive, but the stability of its component plant species will allow it to withstand the rigours of the environment. You need to water the vegetable patch, but not the scrub patch. So if the scrub patch can be made pleasurable, you have solved your problems. It is really as simple as that. Ground hugging and covering plants like *Berberis* and *Cotoneaster* are worth their weight in gold to the wild gardener.

The fact is that the sort of garden many people struggle to maintain demands hard work. To try to keep a patch in a state of arrested development is to enslave yourself to tyranny. Give in and let your garden grow, but plan the agents of growth so that the end result is agreeable. To reduce work you must accept the idea of continuing change, with a habitat slowly altering year by year. Much easier, and infinitely more interesting.

Most gardens lack diversity, containing a fairly stereotyped range of plants – roses, tulips, privet hedge and so on. But diversity is desirable since the more species there are, the more are ready to adapt themselves to changing conditions. Whatever the disaster, something will survive! But sadly man the gardener is not specially interested in the adaptations and survival of species. Part of his pleasure lies in constant importation and experimentation with ever more exotic species. Worse, he plays genetic games, trying to produce forms which satisfy his aesthetic eye and nose, but do not necessarily fulfil their function of providing nectar and pollen and healthy seed. Man denies the garden community the natural right of determining success in terms of evolutionary trial and error. In a natural community every plant and every animal has its own specific part to play and achieves its position by virtue of its fitness, that is by successfully enduring constant and continuing competition. In a garden its 'jobs' may be denied it, competition may be removed or reduced, so its fitness is not properly tested. That means trouble.

Many of the plants we choose to cherish are unpalatable or under-productive in sustaining food for wildlife. Double roses, dahlias, chrysanthemums are all artificially selected to please gardeners, and are very uninteresting to most insects since they produce so little nectar. Roses please greenfly and leafcutter bees, but they impoverish a garden. Try a few weeds – they are tougher, more beautiful, and provide more food for more insects and birds. Plant a few *Valerian* seeds to flower on your walls and attract butterflies. If you are lucky you may even get a humming bird hawk moth to astonish you with its feeding technique.

Remember that the vast majority of the animals in your garden are so small that they are virtually invisible, but their importance is out of all proportion to their size. The function of these miniature creatures is to break down decaying matter and to recycle it into production. Bundle away fallen leaves and that means no work and no food for the micro-organisms. When 'dead' flowerheads are removed they are denied their proper purpose of seeding and then returning their nutrients to the soil. In a healthy ecosystem, the micro-organisms may account for as much as ninety per cent of the action.

People have curious and rather predictable preferences for certain kinds of animal. Rounded, warm and furry ones like bunny rabbits and teddy bears are liked, the long and pointed ones, the phallic snake shape, less so. We don't like things which stare at us in a speculative way. We like them to stand upright like a penguin, to have flat faces with forward-facing eyes and 'noses' like an owl. We like their offensive weapons to be discreetly veiled, like a cat's claws. On the whole we like creatures which exhibit our own supposed characteristics, and how much we like them depends on how well they fit the stereotype. Such vanity!

Quick movers are suspect. Fast insects are usually predators with unattractive habits. Mosquitoes suck blood; that won't do, as it's our blood. Spiders run across the carpet in a menacing way, they pounce on and suck the goodness out of their prey. That won't do. Bees and ladybirds are all right – they are rounded and furry or coloured and they move at a dignified pace. But moving slowly isn't enough: slugs and snails are slow but slimy – bad news. We have to make a real effort to consider each creature objectively. Yet the more one learns about any animal the more interesting it becomes. There aren't really any baddies or goodies.

A garden without slugs and insects would in fact very soon be chaos. No bug is superfluous and where would the blackbird be without the worm? At least we are on safe ground with the blackbird. Plump and rounded, he is off to a head start in the popularity stakes. One of the three most common land birds in Britain (with the house sparrow and starling) he is an opportunist, exploiting man's liking for gardens. An adaptable bird, he was once a woodland species (and still is in Eastern Europe) but now he inhabits gardens and cultivated country, pushing his success ever further north, already inhabiting the Shetlands and Faroes and pioneering Iceland. Birdtable food must be an important factor in his success as a townie, but he is not finicky, eats almost anything and accepts a variety of nest-sites: those are the prerequisites for any species wanting to do well nowadays.

Some animals seem almost to have been programmed to become a success at living with man. The house sparrow, that all-round bird, is even capable of adapting to the city life, and that gives him an edge on most other animals. Like the blackbird and the starling he is an opportunist, but he is more versatile. With the agility of a tit he plunders peanut feeders, he climbs trees using his tail as a foot like a woodpecker, he hawks insects like a house martin.

His association with man is close and long-standing. As a seed-eater he benefited from the grass and cereal growing activities of agricultural man. He soon learnt to colonise houses, finding safe, warm nest-sites and joining the fowls for the morning feed. He happily took to bread and cake as an acceptable version of corn. He finds food easy to come by all through the year so he doesn't need to accumulate fat to power him on migration. He chooses a wife and occupies the same nest-site for life, and that makes for comfort. He is a sedentary creature of set ways.

But he is not a friendly character and he is not a special favourite. He keeps us at arm's length.

The sparrow is a tough customer – however hard you try you won't defeat him. So long as there is food for the taking, the sparrow will be there to take it. Best to learn to live with him. And as the most representative of those commensal species which have learnt to live with us, sparrows are fascinating. They operate in gangs, terrorising other small birds and taking what they want simply by being aggressive, in the best mafia tradition. Scorning the rituals of territorial display and song, they just move in where and when they want. A house martin's nest or blue tit's nestbox suits very well and the rightful occupant is turfed out without ceremony. But they take great care to nest out of your reach within convenient reach of a food supply. They enjoy the free time which goes with their success in a highly sociable atmosphere: sparrow gangs go in for communal dust bathing and animated conversation. A truly remarkable species, but much too clever to be popular.

The most interesting case of a woodland bird coming to terms with

The robin, tailor-made for garden life. This individual is an albino (*Anthony Gibbs*)

the human homestead is that of the robin. On the continent he is a shy, elusive bird. Here, although he remains independent, he has learnt to take advantage of us, and is tailor-made for gardens. As an eater of worms, grubs and insects he welcomes the continual digging and disturbance of the soil. He follows us round as we dig and fork just as once he probably followed the wild boar as it snuffled and snouted and turned over the British soil; we make an acceptable substitute!

There is a whole catalogue of species which originated in the woods and emerged to join us in the garden: jays and tits, woodpeckers and hedgehogs, foxes and badgers. One of the best things about long-term garden-watching is that we can learn to recognise individuals and follow their life stories as they unfold parallel with our own. Birds and mammals, like ourselves, only look alike superficially and usually you can quickly spot the plumage or behaviour differences which distinguish A from B. How much we benefit nowadays from the more sympathetic and constructive attitude which people have towards our wild fellow-inhabitants. As a child I remember only too clearly incidents of brutal cruelty to creatures like frogs and hedgehogs. Nowadays who would throw stones at a hedgehog?

But what of the pleasure of garden-watching? There is the aesthetic appeal of the colour and movement of animals, the desire to know more about the lives of our fellows, the study of numbers, distribution and life style, the collector's instinct for amassing a tally list of species, the fun of watching acrobatics, the pleasure of listening to birdsong and fox bark. All these and more besides. Perhaps it is all just a sublimation of the hunting instinct: we photograph and observe as a substitute for the chase ending in a bloody meal. Call it what you will. For myself I take great joy in actively seeking out all those pleasures.

# 2 WINDOW ON THE WORLD

Look out through the garden window. If you're lucky, you have an open lawn of grass, and maybe a pond, bordered by paths or terraces, bounded by a jungle of shrubs and a backdrop of trees. It is a stage, set for colourful and resounding continuous performance. It is difficult to over-dramatise the whole thing, for in truth all wild life is here, before your very eyes. Stay at home to see the song and dance of territorial combat; the delicate saga of courtship and embrace; the joys of family life and the struggle for survival; above all the constant necessity to feed and to avoid being fed upon.

The backcloth and the performance change as the seasons pass, and the scenes played daily are influenced by wind and weather and by your own activities as the dominant character. But the grand plan is dominated most of all by the existence of two players without whom the entire show would be cancelled once and for all: the soil and the sun. Without the sun there would be no light and warmth, and without their stimulus the ingredients in the soil would never generate life.

Soil is not 'dirt'. The thin layer of soil which covers our planet is a world of its own, with its own atmosphere and water system. Its composition depends on the underlying rock, or the gravels and silts which have been carried by ice or river in the past. Its structure has a great influence on the plants and animals which inhabit it.

The shape and size of the soil particles is of great significance, for the underground inhabitants spend their lives in the spaces between the crumbs. The amount of air in the soil depends on the amount of water in the soil, for air can only occupy the spaces left vacant of water, so drainage is clearly important. Indeed, that dark world is as complex in the interrelationships between its minute plants and animals as is our more familiar world on the surface. In that subterranean world, too, there are representatives of the great divisions – carnivores, herbivores and decomposers – a galaxy of strange and unfamiliar forms like mites and springtails. Their small size bears no relationship to their importance. They form an unseen workforce of mighty proportions, breaking down plant debris, dead bodies and the droppings of bigger beasts, and maintaining a healthy soil balance, fit to support the living world of plants and animals.

Soil varies a great deal according to locality, of course, and where you live will determine, for example, whether your garden is based on chalk or peat and in turn your soil type will have much influence on the wildlife in your garden. If you live on an acid soil you'll have fewer slugs and snails, so you may have fewer hedgehogs. On a sandy well-drained soil, you may be joined by badgers because they find it easy to dig – a mixed blessing.

Most of the soil creatures are so small that you need a microscope to see them. But not all. Dig a spadeful and the first movement will probably come from a worm. If by mischance you have cut it into two parts you will see a fascinating piece of behaviour: one half will wriggle violently and draw attention to itself, while the other quietly worms its way out of sight. Had you been a blackbird you would have been attracted by the wriggling half, thus giving the other part more chance of escape. The point is that, although the segments of a worm are to a certain extent independent of each other, each carrying a set of muscles, excretory organs and nerve branches, the reproductive system is only carried by a few segments and those are the ones which creep unobtrusively away in the hope of escaping the blackbird to live and reproduce, another day, while the wriggling half offers itself as a sacrifice.

Worms only thrive in moist soil. They have no lungs, but 'breathe' all over the body surface. In dry conditions they suffocate, which is why you find very few of them in dry sandy or gravelly soils, but they can survive a long time soaked in water. They are well designed for their job of burrowing, with no awkward projecting limbs. Of the couple of dozen different British species, half-a-dozen are found in soil (others are in places like dung heaps or mudbanks.) Of these, some push the tunnelling spoil into cavities as they go along and some eject the spoil into the outside world, making those castings which irritate so many lawn fanciers. But they should be welcomed, because the soil is turned and aerated, new minerals are brought to the surface, and the improved soil structure helps the process of germination and growth of seeds. There are more worms under a lawn than there are in flower borders because they don't like disturbance; in fact one Danish researcher came to the astonishing conclusion that the weight of earthworms under a farm pasture might be greater than the weight of livestock grazing on it!

Worm populations are much affected by temperature and humidity; the species which makes those lawn casts actually has a resting period during high summer when individuals curl up and opt out till the damper weather of late summer makes life more tolerable. On moist nights at that time they emerge to look for a mate. Although worms are hermaphrodite, carrying both male and female organs, they nevertheless exchange sperm. Lying alongside each other they secrete a tube of mucus which envelops their anterior ends and binds them together. The sperm flows from the testes of each partner as they exchange life one with the other.

For the more mundane business of feeding they will come to the surface to graze. As winter approaches and leaves begin to fall, they go on safari at night in search of willow and cherry leaves and twigs to drag back home, sometimes piling them several inches high. After this dangerous outing they feed from the safety of the burrow.

Although worms have been known to live for ten years in captivity, their wild lives must be much shorter since a whole regiment of creatures preys on them. Practically every bird that gets the chance will eat them, not to mention badgers, hedgehogs, frogs, toads, snakes, carnivorous insects and numerous parasites. No wonder they burrow underground, though even there they can fall to the mole.

Worms are blind and deaf, but very sensitive to vibrations. The approach of a mole may send them post-haste to the surface to face the birds. If you are ever fortunate enough to see a mole at work, or rather to see a molehill erupting as a result of the unseen mole's efforts, watch closely to see if worms erupt as well as a result of the bad vibes.

If the underground vibrations of an approaching mole may cause the worm to surface, perhaps the act of thumping the ground from above may have the same effect: that would explain why we so often see rooks and gulls paddling up and down, walking hard on the same spot. Perhaps the vibrations do the trick, or perhaps the collapse of the soil structure deprives the worm of air. Whatever the reason, there's no doubt that this is a successful worming technique for the crow family and for gulls.

The mole has small eyes and very poor eyesight, but makes up with extra sensitivity to touch and vibration, feeling his way along in the dark with great aplomb. You may never actually set eyes on one, but you can hardly have missed the evidence that moles are about. Those neat little piles of spoil earth have caused a lot of aggro in bowlers, cricketers and lawn over-enthusiasts, so for all his reticence the mole is a much persecuted beast. At one time there was a price on his warm velvety coat, when countrymen wore moleskin trousers, but now he pays the price simply for offending our sense of tidiness. His best chance of a quiet life is when he sets up home in woodland where his mounds are lost among the bracken and the litter of dead wood and leaves.

His down-to-earth name comes from the Old English word molde – dust – so we have moldewarp, the earth-thrower. He naturally prefers light loose soil, even though that may produce fewer worms, but he is provided with powerful tools for his trade. To make passage easier, his appendages are somewhat on the short side, but the forelegs are built like a navvy's, with hands which scrape and lever him through the soil, aided by his equally powerful neck muscles. As the work progresses, the mole turns and pushes the spoil back down the tunnel and it erupts in volcano-style to form the cast which decorates the lawn. So the molehill is actually a by-product, with no value to the mole. In certain conditions a mole may tunnel so close to the surface that his route can be clearly seen as a ridge almost breaking ground; in this case there will be no molehills, but the mole doing this is asking for trouble from birds which might attack him. Less dangerous, from his point of view, will be the robin or blackbird which might follow his progress in the hope of reaping the occasional worm which erupts in panic.

*Moles the crumbled Earth in Hillocks raise.*

John Gay

The only molehill which has a useful purpose marks the mole's nesting place; he throws up one particularly large cast which is known as a fortress. From this home base he patrols his underground territory taking a tithe of the insects and worms. Life is an unending search for food. No time for hibernation in winter – just constant foraging. But if hunting is good, he may store a great quantity of worms in the fortress, biting them so that they are disabled – still alive but unable to get away. When he eats one he carefully wipes it clean with his claws. Drought is his enemy, as it is for the earthworms; moist friable soil is good for both worms and moles. Both ought to be welcome inhabitants of any lawn, but it takes a very tolerant gardener to endure casts whether they're made by mole or worm. Try to look on the bright side of their activities. Use the finely graded soft earth for potting; spread the rest with a rake or a piece of wire netting and think of the good it's doing to your lawn, and consider the innumerable bugs such as cockchafer grubs which the mole is devouring.

You will be lucky to see a mole, unless he should be sick, but they do sometimes show above ground at dusk or in the night collecting grasses and leaves for the nest. In the summer the young moles turfed

Robin, worm and mole: lunchtime co-operative

out into the world are sometimes seen as they seek vacant territory.

Earthworms and moles are permanent residents of the soil, but many other creatures are seasonal occupants. Some insects live part of their lives underground in the larval stage – leather-jackets, the larvae of the crane-fly or daddylonglegs for instance. The adult is fragile, but the grub is a tough customer and an infestation of them may sicken your grass. Deposited as little black eggs in the soil by the female crane-fly, they soon hatch and start to munch grass roots, the bane of farmers and lawn fanciers alike, thriving especially in mild damp winters. After pupating, they emerge as the familiar daddylonglegs in the spring.

The soil is host to many other larvae, like the white morsel of meat which is a cockchafer grub. Helpless and immobile at this stage, it is easy prey for moles and shrews and for the birds which search from above. Rooks and starlings in noisy sociable flocks will quarter a field of grass or a lawn probing for the juicy larvae, aerating and fertilising your lawn at the same time. That's one good turn the starling does. A party of birds busily working over every square inch of your lawn is a measure of the thriving life tucked away below and out of sight, a community which is wholly useful and, indeed, essential for our own existence up on top.

While the bird's technique is moderately genteel, the badger simply excavates a sample of soil, extracting all the worms and grubs he can find. He is particularly fond of a bee's nest. Bumble bees commonly nest under grass or moss and the badger will eat bees, grubs, cocoons, wax, honey and pollen – the lot. Bumble bees like to rest in a field mouse's disused nest-ball; they don't burrow themselves. After hibernation, the queen greets spring by collecting pollen and packing it into a waxy cell into which she lays her eggs. These hatch into grubs, eat the pollen, pupate and hatch into worker bees. The colony reaches its peak in midsummer and in autumn all die except for a few young queens which hibernate to renew the process the following spring. It is fairly easy to encourage bumble bees to take up residence in much the same way that tits will take to nestboxes. Find an old mouse nest (from under a corrugated iron sheet cunningly left on the ground in a suitable corner for instance) and bury it at ground level under a stone or roof tile which keeps the ground dry. Proof the construction against a mouse take-over by covering with half-inch wire netting.

Mining bees are mostly solitary creatures looking much like small honey bees. They make nest cells in sand or earth in lawns, and one species, *Andrena arnata*, makes a little conical pile of earth to mark the entrance. The tunnel may be a couple of feet long, filled from the bottom with a line of nest cells containing eggs and the ready supply of instant grub-growth, pollen. The whole process is over and done with by the end of June and, on the credit side, mining bees are most useful as fruit tree pollinators.

Artificial and man-made though it may be, the green sward of a lawn, clearly observable and yet a constant attraction to bug, beast and bird, is a boon to the naturalist-gardener. Curious that this green invitation to laze and relax is the result of brutal treatment of a inoffensive plant. The constant cutting down of its efforts to reach maturity is hard on the grass and to add insult to injury, we cart off the cuttings to rot elsewhere, depriving the lawn of the very nutrients including nitrogen and lime which help its survival. Of course these are replenished to a certain extent by the activity of soil bacteria and by the constant efforts of worms, but over the years mowing will impoverish the soil if you deny it the cuttings. That is why, if you want to avoid bare patches, you need to import manures to counteract nitrogen deficiency. Again if you cut too often and too close you will be providing conditions favourable to ground-hugging plants like dandelions, daisies and plantains. So give the grass a chance and keep the 'weeds' in the shade, which doesn't suit them at all.

> *There are fairies at the bottom of our garden.*
>
> *'Fairies and chimneys'* Rose Fyleman (*1877–1957*)

Most of the weeds which colonise a lawn are not very popular, but some of the species of fungus are at least spectacular. You may be lucky enough to have the field mushroom growing in fairy rings, especially if you graze a pony on the lawn and it is amply fertilised with horse dung. Puff balls are common on lawns and are perfectly edible, though you should remove the skin before cooking. Eat them while they are young and white, long before they reach the exploding stage. But perhaps the most attractive of lawn fungi is the mushroom *Marasmius oreades*. This is the culprit responsible for those dark and mysterious fairy rings on lawns – marks which remain long after the mushrooms have disappeared. An insubstantial phenomenon, the mushroom is a couple of inches high and a bit wider, with a fragile stem only about an eighth of an inch in diameter. Other species produce rings but this one, common in summer and spring, is most likely to surprise your lawn. The performance starts from a central point and grows outwards like the ripples from a stone thrown in a pond, each specimen producing formidable quantities of spores. The mycelium – the underground portion – persists after the overground ripple has passed by; indeed it lasts for many years. As time goes by chemical action in the soil has a manuring effect and stimulates the grass to ever more luxuriant growth, again in the ripple form, but as the fungus ring expands, year by year, its filament roots choke the air spaces in the soil. Rain water cannot drain through properly and the grass is deprived at the very time its healthy growth is demanding a good supply of water. The virtual drought kills the grass and soon there is a bare ring (where the fairies dance) inside the still flourishing and expanding mushroom ring, firmly based on the unseen but vital mycelium. In time, as the mushroom ring expands still further, the inner clogging mycelium dies, the rain penetrates once again and life begins anew for the grass.

> *Here the horse-mushrooms make a fairy ring,*
> *Some standing upright and some overthrown,*
> *A small stonehenge, where heavy black snails cling*
> *And bite away like Time, the tender stone.*

'*The Fairy Ring*' Andrew Young

Lawn-watching is the easiest way of discovering some of the different adaptations and techniques used by birds for feeding. One of the constant wonders of the natural world is its diversity, the extraordinary range of plants and animals in any given habitat, and the way they all manage to make a living by occupying slightly different niches. Superficially the 'nature red in tooth and claw' approach may seem justified, but it would be more just to see communities of different creatures living in tolerable harmony. Birds come in all shapes and sizes. Some hunt by day, some by night. Some are vegetarian, some are meat-eaters, some eat anything they can get hold of, including other birds. Some walk after their food, some hop for it, some fly for it, some dive and swim for it. And each is specially equipped for the chosen job. One way or another anything which grows or moves gets eaten by something. Fruit, nuts, seeds, leaves, bark, living matter and decaying matter, all is grist to the mill.

Very roughly we can divide birds into four categories according to the shape of their beaks: the hard-billed birds like sparrows or finches which have nutcracker bills; the soft-billed birds like robins which deal with insects; the dual purpose bills which take on all comers; and the hook-billed predators like sparrow hawks.

On the lawn, the most obvious visitors are the birds searching for worms and soft grubs. The old saying about the early bird getting the worm is an exact observation of fact. Worms are creatures of moisture and mildness; early morning dew suits them, sunrise and sun warmth does not and they retire underground. So thrushes and blackbirds comb the lawn at first light and this is when you may see the bigger blackbird steal worms from the song thrush, getting his breakfast the easy way.

Birds have a well-developed sense of hearing, but they hunt almost entirely by the use of sight, and to some extent touch; at least that is true of those most active by day. When the thrush catches a worm, he does it because he has seen it first. The longstanding mis-observation that birds listen for worms is based on a characteristically human weakness: people make the classic mistake of regarding birds, or any other animal for that matter, as if they too were people. The worm-hunting thrush hops a few paces, then stands very still and cocks its head to one side. A pause, and then the stab. So we deduce that the bird had its head cocked to listen for the sound of the worm. But the observation failed to take note of the fact that the bird's *eye* happens to be in the position where the human *ear* is found. When a man cocks his head in that attitude, he is listening intently; when a thrush does it, he is watching intently.

People are strangely slow to believe that bird sight is an improvement on their own. I am often asked by what strange sixth sense birds know that a particular delicacy has been thrown onto the lawn for them. Why are distant seagulls so quick to respond to scraps of meat and fat but take their time for stale bread, they ask. But the answer is simple: gulls can see what is on offer as well as you can, but from a greater distance. And what's more, when one gull is excited about a find, his very behaviour in flying down to it attracts distant gulls. Seabirds like gulls and, more spectacularly, gannets, can keep in touch with the news over large expanses of sea by watching each other. This, incidentally, accounts for their white plumage. Other species may have drab camouflage, but seabirds have fewer predators and don't mind being seen.

Woodland species like buzzards can see a beetle from hundreds of feet in the air. Certainly it isn't the sense of smell that's used; birds *can* smell, but apparently do not use this ability. Sight – and sometimes sound – is what is important.

As it is the early bird which catches the worm, starlings tend to miss out on the morning feast. Roosting in city centres outside the breeding season, they tend to arrive late on the lawn scene, and will be probing for leather-jackets and insect grubs, as well as picking up the kitchen scraps. They are much maligned; if they were rare we should be delighted to see them. In breeding plumage they fully justify their name – little star. Their sociable habits and skill as mimics just do not seem to be able to make up for their supposed bullying character in the bird-garden. One of the problems of success!

The bird which is a universal favourite when he swoops onto the lawn is the green woodpecker, with his striking green plumage and red head. His curious flight – a few flaps followed by a glide with wings clasped tight to body – and yaffling call bring him switchbacking into the garden. So remarkable is his appearance that many people can't believe he is a British bird at all, working on the dismal assumption that home-grown species are bound to be dull and dowdy! But British he is, and a delight to see, working over the lawn and exploring for ants and ant nests. The other woodpeckers, equally striking in their red and white livery, are less attracted to ground level, but the green wood-pecker, with his long, mobile tongue tipped with sticky mucus,

The green woodpecker's extensible tongue

searches out larvae from their hidey-holes in crevices. He may spear out larger bugs and grubs, but ants are his speciality. In hard weather when ants are scarce he may become a nuisance to bee-keepers by breaking and entering hives to eat the bees; and he may vandalise nestboxes by enlarging the tit-sized holes in order to gain entry to search for bugs inside.

Some of the lawn visitors are looking for grass and weed seeds, and of these perhaps the most attractive is the goldfinch. The sight of a charm of goldfinches attacking the golden dandelions ought to be enough to convert any gardener into a dandelion fan. They approach them with zest, leapfrogging onto the stems, landing about half way up towards the head so that they weigh it down to the ground. Then they get to work. All finches are seed-eaters, with powerful jaw muscles and bills modified for husking. They have two grooves inside the bill which locate the nut or seed, then the tongue rotates it as the mandibles crush. The husk peels off, leaving the kernel to be swallowed. Different finches go for different seeds, a hawfinch for example is tough enough to cope with cherry and plum stones. Goldfinches, at the weaker end of the finch scale, use their relatively long narrow bills rather like a pair of tweezers, probing deep into the seedhead.

Even a magpie will weigh down a plant stem to attack the seedhead, and is representative of those birds which will eat almost anything, including other birds and eggs if it gets the chance. It has even been alleged to lift dustbin lids to get at the contents.

Swallows will occasionally settle on a lawn to pick up flies, but most of the time they are concerned with airborne flies. Their beaks are wide and flattened, designed to scoop quantities of insects out of the air. With their forked tail streamers they are easy to distinguish from the white-rumped house martins, although they may mix together as they feed in the air space above your garden. But the swift is the most completely aerial bird, in this country anyway. He not only catches his food on the wing but he mates, and probably even sleeps, in flight. Indeed he would probably never touch down at all if it weren't impossible to incubate an egg while airborne. Perhaps in the course of evolution he will manage that, as may many seabirds which would never come ashore if only they could make a nest on the surface of the sea. The swift flies from near ground level up to 1,000 feet, grazing the insect pastures of the air, and filling it with those screams which nostalgically recall continental holidays. Like the swallow, he has a big head and a wide mouth with bristles round it, designed to act like an aerial shrimp net.

A bird's bill is in effect its hand, useful in picking up and preening operations, but most important as an implement for handling food. The mandibles are horny sheaths, rather like our finger nails, but based on the jawbone; like finger nails, they are growing all the time, so normal wear and tear is continually compensated. Cage birds, like budgies, which do not get enough work, sometimes have to have their 'nails' cut. If a bird damages a mandible, the sheath regenerates in its own good time, although there may be deformities. In this situation a bird's survival may depend on its adaptability, for a damaged bill may make life very difficult for an over-fastidious feeder. Abnormally shaped beaks are not uncommon, however, and these may have nothing to do with damage or injury. Starlings in particular seem sometimes to grow curlew-shaped bills as much as $2\frac{1}{2}$ inches long for instance, possibly an inherited genetic phenomenon. They are easy-going birds prepared to make a meal of anything edible, and seem to manage well enough. This sort of bill abnormality is common in the cage-bird world, where aviculturalists tend to think incorrect feeding is to blame.

Sometimes exotic visitors arrive in gardens: escaped cage birds may turn up to puzzle and confuse the local birdwatchers; budgies or canaries will visit a birdtable for weeks or even months in the summer. The harsh weather of winter usually finishes them, even if they survive the sparrowhawks and crows, but there are some astonishing success stories, like the rose-ringed parakeets which have established themselves all around London and are keen visitors to the birdtables for peanuts. Mild winters certainly help them.

Perhaps the most spectacular lawn visitor, but one that you're only likely to see if you live on the south coast, is the hoopoe. With its pinkish-brown plumage, barred black on the wings and back, it swoops in to the grass with a lazy flight. On landing it shows a remarkable crest in the shape of a fan, pink with black tips. Then it struts about, probing into the soil with its long curved bill. Typically, it prefers parkland, orchard and open wooded country, but it is fond of the vicinity of houses, where it feeds on lawns and paths for insect larvae. A very few stay with us to nest, in holes in trees or buildings, and some years there is a considerable influx of them, so keep an eye open. One of the hoopoe's most endearing traits is its tameness and tolerance of man; even the French are fond of it and refrain from shooting it. It gets its name from its voice – a low, but penetrating sexy hoop-oop-oop. The scientific name is *Upupa epops* – both onomatopoeic and charming!

Voices are important to animals, exactly as they are to us, for communication and information. Birds, for instance, are largely dependent on sight for finding food, but when it comes to finding a mate the first requirement is a voice. In the battle for home and family, much effort goes into signalling of one kind and another, but the most important displays are visual and aural.

> On a tree by a river a little tom-tit
> Sang 'willow, tit willow, tit willow!'
> And I said to him, 'Dicky-bird, why do you sit
> Singing 'willow, tit willow, tit willow?'.

'*The Mikado*' W. S. Gilbert

Birdsong may be enjoyable for us to listen to, but the birds are not singing to please us! Of course language has various functions, and one kind of call (like the familiar churr of a jay for instance) may give warning that a predator is about. It is disseminating information. Another call may serve to keep a group of birds in touch. Yet another kind may involve the language of love, person to person, bird to bird. But first and foremost we have to deal with full-throated song, proclaimed from the top of a tree, where the bird is positively drawing attention to itself.

> Sumer is icumen in,
> Lhude sing cuccu

'*Cuckoo Song*' Anon *c1226*

This kind of behaviour, on the face of it, is so monumentally stupid, exposing the bird to the attentions of all its enemies, that there has to be a powerful justification. It must have survival value. Well, an Englishman's home may seem to be his castle, but it's actively defended by a whole host of other creatures each regarding it, in deadly seriousness, as uniquely *their* home. They defend it, and have an urgent need to perpetuate their species in it. And that is the nub of the matter: the principle function of birdsong is to proclaim a territory and to attract a mate.

In winter most birds are too busy to sing, and many of our breeding species are away in foreign parts. But as the sap begins to rise, so do the testosterone levels in the cock bird's blood. His aggressive instincts refuelled, he turns his mind to land ownership and the acquisition of a mate. So, as light percolates the morning garden, it triggers a dawn chorus of naked aggression and lust.

Each species has its own distinctive 'brand image', an identifiable song. Warblers, finches, tits, thrushes – dozens of different species each with a clearly distinctive call, conveying the basic information – species and sex. And each individual within a species is clearly distinguishable by his fellows.

'That's the wise thrush; he sings each song twice over' wrote Browning. Good observation, that is. The song thrush does tend to repeat each phrase twice, sometimes three times, and perhaps the best poetic version of the thrush call is: 'Summer is coming, summer is coming, I know it, I know it, I know it!' (Tennyson). The poets have rendered the song into plain English, but what does it mean? What is the thrush actually singing? When he gets up and opens his mouth the news comes pealing out. 'It is spring and the sap has risen. I am a cock song thrush, I am in full breeding condition. I warn all male song thrushes that I own this patch and will defend it against all comers with my life. I hereby advertise for a female song thrush to present herself. Should we suit each other, I shall invite her to live with me and be my love, sharing this desirable property with suitable nest-sites.'

Now the effect of that broadcast depends on who is within reception range. A chiffchaff will ignore it, a robin will ignore it. A cock song thrush will prick up his ears and bristle, recognising the challenge and the opportunity. A female song thrush, if she's already suited, will ignore it. An unpaired thrush, clearly understanding the invitation, may approach closer. If no song thrush is within audible distance, nothing will happen and the incumbent male will continue to advertise. He will sing from somewhere effective, the top of a tree or the top of a telegraph pole. Either will do – indeed from his point of view they are both trees anyway, though one is a particularly poor specimen for purposes other than a songpost. What he wants is a commanding view and the biggest potential audience.

Not all birds sing from the top of a tree or a rooftop. Skylarks live in open country. But they solve the problem in the most elegant fashion, taking to the wing and singing from an invisible songpost in the sky. Many birds are reluctant to leave the dense cover of the shrubbery, but for them too what more effective way of conveying the message than by singing? Down on the lawn the grasshopper has this same problem of living in a dense medium, but he does the best he can, climbing to the top of a grass stem to increase his range and chirping out his message by rubbing his leg to and fro along the serrated edge of his wing. Some birds, too, do not produce their song vocally: woodpeckers, for instance, find themselves a tree with a good ringing acoustic, and then rap smartly with rapid blows of the bill, so drumming out the immortal message. Less poetically they'll even tap out the message on the junction box of a television aerial on someone's roof!

Swallows and swifts are aerial species, but they often breed communally and share territorial air space. A mole's patch is underground, centering on the nest fortress and spreading out along the tunnels which may reach out as much as 150 yards. He makes no territorial claims on the land or air above. Territories may overlap amongst different species, but that is not significant. They matter between individuals of the same species, and in essence they represent a defended area. Territories are not necessarily defended at all times. Robins, for example, are very keen on land ownership, staking claim after the summer moult and keeping it it right through winter to the breeding season. They are unsociable creatures – you only see them in groups on Christmas cards. Unless they are actually paired, robins will not tolerate companionship. The song is loud and continuous – 'keep off'. At the other end of the scale, a goldfinch may only establish his claim just before building a nest and even then the defended ground consists only of the area in which he nests and mates, just a few square yards. Different species, different attitudes.

> *One bushe can not harbour two Robin redbreasts.*

Proverb *1583*

What happens when the singer is challenged? Sometimes a bird which understands the significance of the song nevertheless decides to call the bluff in the hope of usurping the prize. The challenger approaches closer, deliberately invading the territory. And he sings. The two sing at each other in a slanging match. The invader comes closer, till there is an eyeball-to-eyeball confrontation. Once in visual contact they bring weapons other than song to bear. The splendid breeding plumage is displayed in all its glory, each bird presenting itself to the best advantage, fluffing itself up to look bigger. Both posture and strut in an overbearing manner – Mr World incarnate. Mammals use the same methods: a badger will fluff his coat up so that he looks twice

A slanging match: starling and aggressive song thrush (*Eric Hosking*)

his size. He will lower his head to show the black and white danger stripes for the full benefit of his opponent. Badger or bird will use its recognition marks to make the point. And it is important to remember that these plumage or fur patterns are brought into play on different occasions for different purposes. The colours and patterns may at one time be used to attract and at another to repel.

Aggressive postures are a part of everyday life for all of us, part of the struggle to corner the best food, the best roosting place, the best territory and the best partner. But for birds they are most important in spring. Lengthening days make the task of finding food easier and allow more spare time but, most important, it is the onset of the breeding season. The birdtable is a likely place to see the action. Blackbirds which previously met there in peace will suddenly take to posturing and vocal threats, becoming uneasy when another bird is within a critical distance. A cock chaffinch will not tolerate another cock chaffinch close to him at this time, yet they spend the winter in an all-male club of great tolerance and camaraderie.

In a typical threatening situation a bird will thrust its head forward or upward and show its breast feathers boldly to its opponent. The feathers fluff out and it will spread its wings, perhaps showing off the colourful secondaries. The object of the exercise is to go through the motions of starting a fight but decidedly not to advance to the stage of combat. The hope is for a speedy stand-down by one of the contestants, long before the bell rings for the first round and mostly this is what happens. One of the sparring partners brings the affair to a speedy end by crouching down submissively with his head withdrawn and his feathers almost relaxed. The only damage is to his pride, and he promptly goes to elaborate lengths to display to the world at large that he was only joking really – nothing serious – and that had he wanted to he could have wiped the floor with his opponent. He engages busily in some unnecessary and irrelevant activity like preening, or pretending to feed.

*'Let's fight till six, and then have dinner', said Tweedledum.*

*'Alice through the Looking Glass'* Lewis Carroll

This 'displacement activity' is rather like ear-scratching in humans – an effort to distract attention from a problem. In a confused situation in which fighting is possible, birds may peck the ground, pull out a beakful of grass, do almost anything to substitute for the activity they want to avoid. A popular-feeding area may find half a dozen pairs of blackbirds calling each other names and squaring up for interminable mock battles. Anything which produces an agreed winner and loser without bloodshed is acceptable. But threats have to be faced, and this leads to some comic situations, as when blackbirds sing and posture at a car mirror or hubcap, or a garden window, believing their own image to be that of an intruder. This sort of behaviour is only evident during the breeding season.

Actual physical assault leading to grievious bodily harm only happens in territorial battles when all else has failed. Singing, posturing, screaming, making faces and chasing are all preliminaries to the fight, but even if they actually get to grips with each other there's usually more noise than damage. The consequences of actual damage are too serious, for an injured bird is in real and instant danger. At worst, the protagonists will lock themselves in open combat, pecking and clawing, until one capitulates in flight and an ignominious exit. Fights are not always entirely mock, and indeed in rare cases they may end in tragedy. The result of one battle observed between rival blue tits ended in death, with the loser's skull dented like a collapsed table-tennis ball.

> For he who fights and runs away
> May live to fight another day;
> But he who is in battle slain
> Can never rise and fight again.

'Art of Poetry on a New Plan' Oliver Goldsmith (1728–1774)

But our hero's problems are not over when he has fought his fight and established himself as king of the castle. Even when his choice is made and he turns his attentions to dalliance, the road is far from clear. Courtship, as we all know, is fraught with problems. Most animals, including ourselves, tend to shy away from actual touch most of the time, but perpetuation of the species requires physical contact. So to overcome that natural reserve there is the ritual of courtship. And the object of the ritual, no matter what the species, is to permit approach and copulation.

There is much anxiety, tension and fear to overcome and the very apparatus of aggression and combat are now employed to a totally different end. The screaming of land-grab becomes the language of love. The gorgeous colours of the plumage and facial expressions continue the process. Music and movement become the billing and cooing of love. But the mating situation is so fraught with conflicting emotions that one wonders that it ever results in success. For while the cock bird is pressing attentions on a hen, he may be distracted by a rival cock singing. He must break off one kind of engagement to enter another, using the same weapons for opposite purposes. No wonder the interval between the first meeting and the consummation is sometimes prolonged.

Pairing may take place well before Christmas in many species, but the first couple of months of the New Year are usual. The sexes instantly recognise each other, difficult though that may seem to us in cases where, male and female, their plumage is identical, as in the robin or wood pigeon.

When two male wood pigeons meet, the tenant usually wins the mock battle, possession being nine-tenths of the law. The intruder may have to be jostled a bit, but he goes. But if the visitor is a female, she stands firm, albeit rather uneasily, while the male bows courteously, showing his white and green neck patches and his white wing bars to best advantage. He will sing his 'tak two coos, taffy' routine, or he will exhibit a short soaring display flight, with a spectacular stall and a clap of his wings. The female may stand her ground, or she may retreat a little before the wonder of it all. The male too may be confused, still uncertain whether he is called on to raise his head and stretch his wing tips in threat, or bow his head and raise his tail to convince the female that his intentions are honourable. For her part, she has to be convinced that the male is not going to attack her. And so the bowing continues, the neck is inflated to show the irridescent greens and the Persil-white patches, until they are both reassured and the next phase begins. It may be days before the birds are perching alongside each other on the same branch, billing and cooing their pleasure. Mutual preening will now serve to reinforce the rapidly growing bond. The cock bird will lean across and nibble at the little feathers on her forehead, which stimulates her pituitary gland so that soon she is ready to lay eggs. The sex act itself will be accompanied by much billing and feather-caressing, and the hen may solicit food from the cock in the manner of juveniles begging. This feeding further stimulates copulation and strengthens the pair bond.

Courtship feeding is typical of many species (including man!). You may see a hen robin on the lawn, making the same call she made as a spotty juvenile. She crouches, with wings held down to the ground, quivering, then the cock bird passes a juicy grub to her, a token of his love.

It is not always the males which establish the breeding territory. Among blackbirds, for instance, the females choose the home patch. Mostly the cock birds tend to gather in groups at roosting or bathing time, taking this opportunity to assert themselves and establish seniority. They pull rank on each other, with dancing displays, mock fights, chasing and bowing, chattering away. And as the days go by they direct their attentions more towards the hens. In the New Year pairs begin to emerge and, with bonds acknowledged, they confirm the territory and repel all boarders. Much of this is done before the cock bird begins to sing, a procedure which, untypically, comes late on the agenda, some time in February or March.

Blackbirds, and other species for that matter, may sometimes be

Robins courtship feeding

seen, astonishingly, to mate or attempt to mate with foreign objects like tennis balls or dog's bones lying about on the lawn. This is only the sad evidence of frustration, and the bird is copulating with a substitute partner. Given the arrival in the garden of an unattached female, he will quickly find a more suitable object on which to lavish his all. Such aberrations are examples of 'redirection', a perfectly proper behaviour response directed at an improper subject as when a bird pecks at inedible things as substitutes for the food it really wants, and when a man bangs his desk when what he really wants to do is thump his boss.

Do birds mate for life? Probably most of them do, given the chance. But small birds do not live long so it is the larger ones, like swans, which get the benefit of a reputation for fidelity in marriage. The advantages of life partnership are real. If you already know your mate, then the annual courtship formalities may be reduced, leaving more time and energy for the practical processes and duties of breeding. But it is not easy to be dogmatic about the long-term effectiveness of the pair bond, since the birds may be returning not so much to a known partner as to a known nest-site, where last year's mate is conveniently ready to hand. Certainly there is the bird equivalent of divorce as a result of incompatibility, and if one partner dies, the other will look for a replacement. Common sense normally prevails. There are survival advantages in a successful marriage, so it has an assured future for wild creatures.

Much of what is true for birds is true of mammals and other orders. Carnivores like the fox have their version of territorial song, but they have another very important device: their use of the scent gland. Many mammals live in a world of smells and by marking their territorial boundaries with their own scent they both warn off the opposition and leave an invitation card for the vixen. Their scent is not attractive to us – and it is most persistent. I once had a young fox in the back of my car for a few days, and the effluvium lingered on for well over three months. It is natural enough that a species should prefer its own scent-gland secretion to that of other species. Only the human animal has the extraordinary habit of concealing the smell of its own natural secretions by swamping them with that of some unfortunate exotic cat, which has had its scent glands removed for the benefit of the perfume industry.

Postures and slanging matches are part of the mammal world too. In early spring, you may see grey squirrels chasing and squeaking through the trees and down onto the lawn; buck and doe indulge in a great deal of rough and tumble, rolling about the grass as part of the courtship ritual.

In amongst the jungle of grass and weeds down close to the earthy floor of the lawn, insects will be engaged in the same delightful pursuits. Grasshoppers leap and saw their scratchy songs, worms lock themselves in love, and spiders pursue their love dances. On a sunny day you may see the wolf spider engaged in courtship, with his legs and sensory palps waving a semaphore signal to the lady of his choice. These hunting spiders are very different from the web spiders which sit and wait for their prey. Wolf spiders are active hunters and they have good eyes. So while web spiders approach each other by means of vibration signals along the telegraph lines of the web, the hunters use visual signals, the semaphoring which you see on lawn or windowsill, when they approach each other. The delicacy of the process for all spiders is bound up with the fact that the larger and more powerful female spends most of her life attacking flies, and in the early stages there is always the danger that she might think the approaching hopeful is a fly and treat him accordingly. She does not eat her mate as a deliberate and spooky part of the marriage ceremony as many people think; if she does eat him, it is just the outcome of an unfortunate failure on his part to get his identity and message across.

> *Help me.*
> *I think I'm falling*
> *In love again.*
> *When I get that crazy feeling, I know*
> *I'm in trouble again.*
>
> *Song lyric by* Joni Mitchell

Some animals indulge in spectacular marriage displays, and the garden ant is a good example. On sultry days in high summer, the young males and queens emerge from the comfortable obscurity of the underground nest, accompanied by great numbers of excited workers. While the earthbound workers mill about on the paving stones or the grass, the winged males and queens take to the air for the marriage flight. The impregnated queens then adventure off to found new colonies. The number of insects involved in these flights is prodigious, and as weather conditions are critical the swarms may emerge simultaneously from many gardens in a neighbourhood. Then there will be a spirit of carnival abroad, quickened by the prompt arrival of swallows, house martins and swifts taking advantage of the easy pickings. Sad to think of the joyous flight being so rudely disturbed, but the relationships between hunter and hunted need to be looked at coolly.

The principal fact, and one that many people find hard to accept, is that on the whole the predator/prey relationship is in the best interest of the species being taken. The hunter catches and despatches the slowest and the sickest of his potential victims, leaving the population stronger and the field free for the best specimens to breed. So the relationship may actually *increase* the population of the species, which in any case is affected most of all by the amount of food available. Not every attack results in a kill, of course, and every time an animal escapes he emerges just a little wiser, which is good for his species too. In reverse, the number of predators in any given area is determined by the prey available; only the fittest and fastest hunters survive.

If you see the small birds in your garden 'freeze' suddenly, there will be a predator about, perhaps a squirrel or a magpie. If a sparrowhawk is the cause of it all, he will have come and gone almost before the small birds have time to think about freezing. He flashes through the garden like an avenging angel, just missing the obstacles in a headlong dash and picking off a blue tit or a sparrow in passing, before rocketing off over the hedge. A sparrowhawk may well develop a specialist interest in your birdtable, coming not for the cake but for the tit that's eating it! Many people feel they should defend 'their' birds from the sparrowhawk, but I think it is a healthier attitude to let the birds fight it out amongst themselves. The scientific attitude must be that if the tit is dim enough to be caught then he is not a suitable candidate for protection! A difficult subject.

There is some justification for objecting to the way a grey squirrel acts out his predatory role on the small birds in your garden. After all, he is an interloper, indigenous to North America and very ill-advisedly introduced to this country at the turn of the century. Grey squirrels eat many eggs, and will even enlarge the entrance hole of a nest box in order to extract and eat the nestlings. It is your statutory duty to eliminate them from the garden, but these things are easier said than done. In the States they are a recognised game animal though there can't be much meat on them. They are a very hardy and successful species, and it's difficult not to have a sneaking regard for them, with their acrobatic charm. It's the foresters who hate them most for their destructive habit of ring-barking young hardwood trees.

Cats are a problem; if you have both a cat and a birdtable you are asking for trouble. What is unfair is to blame the cat for doing something it is designed to do – to hunt. And when it is successful, bringing in sad little bundles of fur or feather to display proudly on the carpet,

Kestrel

45

you must grit your teeth and praise it – and hope that it eats the body, because it compounds the sadness if, having lost its small life, the vole or bird does not even have its goodness recycled by its captor.

Much of the interest in garden-watching consists of observing the fitness of design for purpose in the creatures you see, and surely it is best to learn from the drama, rather than decry it. So I believe in leaving sparrowhawks and crows and cats to get on with it, to their several benefits. And I take pleasure in seeing the speed and power of the sparrowhawk, and try not to think too much about the sparrow, in the knowledge that sparrows as a species are in very little danger. Predators tend to have their senses honed to a fine pitch. Not for nothing does a countryman say, when he wants to praise someone, 'Ee've a got the eyes of an 'awk, and the 'earing of an owl.'

Sparrowhawks are seen often enough in gardens, perhaps more often than the commoner kestrel, presumably because the kestrel is adapted for searching out mice and voles in open country. The sparrow-hawk is an expert at picking off small birds in flight in the woods and woodland edge, so he is quickly at home in the garden, especially where many small birds congregate at feeding stations. Certainly he is a significant factor in controlling the numbers of sparrows, tits and finches.

Kestrels are much more at home on the new motorway verges, long open tracts where mice flourish and sparrowhawks would not feel comfortable. They are taking happily to town life, nesting on the window ledges and crevices of high-rise flats, and feeding on house sparrows. Cities have a lot to offer predators, with a large population of pigeons and sparrows, many of them undernourished and easy prey. Maybe soon we shall be seeing the peregrines as common city-centre birds, with eyries on the building-cliffsides, and the tidal ebb and flow of traffic to represent the sea below, and with the familiar rock dove/pigeon to make them feel at home.

Predators don't get it all their own way. Quite apart from the fact that they don't always kill, they are themselves molested by the very birds they prey on. Blackbirds chivvy cats, rooks chivvy buzzards and small birds chivvy owls the moment they show themselves. This 'mobbing' is a form of display, the birds most at risk banding together

Small birds mobbing tawny owl

to call attention to the danger. Hoping to avert attack, they feel there is some safety in numbers.

There are some creatures whose unwelcome attentions affect us more personally. Ants sting, along with wasps, bees, horse-flies and, most tiresomely, mosquitoes. The many species of mosquito which live happily in Britain fortunately spend a great deal of time sucking nectar from flowerheads, but the females, sad to say, also use their hypodermic proboscis to extract our blood. One has to admire the elegant and unobtrusive technique, although I imagine few people go to the length of attracting mosquitoes to the garden pond: they represent just about the only disadvantage of that facility, a lawn without a pond being sadly deficient. At least in the larval stage, mosquitoes don't present any threat to us. The eggs float in rafts, but hatch into larvae which hang from the surface tension, feeding on tiny particles of passing food. Then they pupate into a floating form till eventually the adult emerges, the innocent male to suck nectar, the vicious female to suck our blood as well.

But the last thing I want to do is deter anyone from setting up a garden pond, for it is the source of much pleasure. You may be visited by dragonflies; kingfishers may come to take tadpoles, and the community of life underwater will be a delight. The surface tension supports pond skaters and water crickets on top of it and mosquito and gnat larvae hang from it. In the open water there is room for sticklebacks, newts and plankton creatures, especially if you resist the temptation to introduce those foreign goldfish which muddy the pond. On the bottom, enriched with the particles of decaying plant and animal remains, there will be bugs which can survive in an oxygen-deficient atmosphere – midge larvae and sludge worms. Best of all are the weedy margins of the pond, where pond snails and caddis grubs graze the vegetation, newts and tadpoles forage, water beetles and water boatmen hunt their prey. If you have water lilies, then blackbirds may turn the leaves over and take the flatworm and snail eggs attached to the underside.

You may be lucky enough to see a grass snake come to swim about after tadpoles and frogs: almost everything, including even sparrows, seems to relish a tadpole, and it's no wonder that frogs produce such an extravagant cloud of spawn. Even when they're grown up and leave the pond for the cool grass, frogs are in constant danger from hedgehogs, stoats, weasels, badgers, otters, rats, owls and herons, not to mention the grass snake, whose main food item is the frog. No wonder they are good jumpers. On top of that list of enemies they have been much persecuted by toxic chemicals. Garden ponds may now be an important factor in their survival.

*A frog he would a-wooing go*
*Heigh ho! says Rowley.*

*Nursery rhyme quoted in 'Melismata'* (1611) Thomas Ravenscroft

48

Frogs may begin their courtship as early as January, although the season goes through to March according to the area. They may be a long way from the pond when the sap begins to rise, resting the winter away in a nice muddy hole somewhere and their cross-country journey may be quite spectacular. Even if there are other ponds about, they'll choose to go to the same one each year, crossing roads and fields on the way if necessary. That's when vast numbers of frogs and toads get killed by motor cars. A warm wet night is the best time to see them. And how do they find their way to the home pond? Probably by its smell, its own unique effluvium, wafted down the wind.

The males are first to get there and they are the croakers. They can even croak underwater, because they make the noise by shuttling air back and forth between lungs and mouth. The females arrive to a warm embrace, which may last nearly twenty-four hours. And there's a great deal of competition. The unmated males get into a frenzy and clutch at anything in their desire for contact. If they clutch at another male, then there is a warning grunt and a prompt disengagement. If it's an ovulating female the male grips her tight. With vents close together the couple form a fertile production line – eggs first, followed

Common frogs mating

by a sprinkling of sperm, and soon the pond is full of spawn clouds. Each female may lay as many as a couple of thousand eggs but it's a lucky egg which hatches into a tadpole which metamorphoses into a frog which lives to enjoy your grassy lawn in the summer. They are entirely useful creatures to welcome in the garden, eating snails by the bucketful.

> *Be kind and tender to the frog*
> *And do not call him names . . .*
>
> 'The Frog' Hilaire Belloc

Toads will use your pond for mating and producing the long egg strings, but they are more choosy than frogs, liking to be down deep. Newts use a different system altogether. The male prepares a parcel of sperm which he delivers to the female in a courtship ritual during which he swishes his tail to create a current, on which an enticing chemical reaches the female, attracting her up-current to the parcel. She picks it up with the lips of her vent, and the sperms reach the eggs inside. The eggs are fertilised internally, an adaptation which turned out to to be convenient for land-dwelling animals, paving the way for pioneer colonisers like slugs and snails, and indeed man himself.

Newts hunt by both sight and smell, chasing aquatic larvae and crustaceans, molluscs, frogspawn and tadpoles. Try dropping a small piece of raw meat into the pond, to find if you have any newts, for they will soon smell it. They will eat almost anything that moves. In mid-summer they leave the pond and come ashore for a spell, and at this time will take earthworms and snails. They seem equally happy in the water or out of it.

Many animals will come to drink and bathe in your pond: birds, grass snakes and slow worms. Hedgehogs will amble over to it and lean in to drink, often enough falling in as well, so it is vital to keep the water-level high and to avoid vertical surfaces, which may defeat even a good climber like a hedgehog if slippery with algae. If the pond is big enough it's a good idea to have an island or raft in the centre, providing a safe place for birds to land. They may also use lily leaves as natural islands. Sparrows have been known to land on a lily leaf, and take a quick bathe as they slowly sink into the water. Swallows may literally drop in to sip and splash as they fly by. It is interesting to compare the drinking requirements of different birds, and the various techniques they use. In areas like the deserts of North America and Australia for instance, species like the desert sparrow or budgerigar can go for long periods without water, even on a dry diet of seeds. But in the British Isles there is no such bird. All of them need water frequently even if, like arboreal species, they get it from drops on leaves after rain. Most small birds take repeated drinks, raising the head each time to

Most birds, like this sparrow, do not enjoy rain . . .

. . . but wood pigeons bathe in it

swallow. But the pigeon, for instance, keeps his head down and imbibes continuously, sucking the water up.

Even if you have no pond, you should provide a bathing and drinking place for the wild animals in your garden, preferably with clear water. For bathing, the water should be shallow – less than two inches deep is best. Birds will even bathe in damp grass, so clearly it is important to them. For many, like the starling, it is a social activity. And they are not bathing simply to clean off dirt. It has a much more serious function, being the necessary preliminary to preening, the process of feather maintenance. Flight is the bird's main survival mechanism, and much time is spent keeping its flying gear fully airworthy.

So after wetting, but not soaking, the plumage, the bird shakes and goes somewhere secure to preen; it is at risk until the feathers are in trim again. Using its beak, it nibbles and strokes the feathers one by one, then shakes them into position. The problem of its head, where the bill cannot reach, is solved by scratching with its foot. Now it fans the tail out to one side, and reaches back to the oil gland, stimulating it with its bill. The oil is then stroked on to the plumage, where it dries.

All these preening motions of stroking, scratching, wing and tail stretching, are highly stereotyped, automatic movements, and they may be seen at times when no serious preening is involved – in leisure time, as part of courtship, or as a displacement activity.

*Waters above! Eternal springs!*
*The dew that silvers the Dove's wings!*

'*The Dove*' Henry Vaughan

Pigeons will actually bathe in rain, leaning over with raised wing, presenting themselves to the rain drops. But most birds, like us, seem more concerned to avoid that kind of wetting. Wet plumage means less flying efficiency. When sitting in the open on a nest, birds will hunch themselves in an attitude which sheds rain as quickly as possible, and there is an astonishing record of a moorhen which deliberately covered itself with a handy plastic sheet to keep dry. This was seen by a photographer who was keeping a close watch on the nest (while staying dry in his hide).

Like many other animals, birds will sunbathe. Possibly their relaxed posture and gaping beaks may indicate heat distress, but there's little doubt that they sunbathe deliberately, probably for a beneficial chemical effect. The ultraviolet rays of the sun shining on the feathers produce vitamin D, subsequently consumed during preening. The warmth of the sun may also stimulate parasites to expose themselves to capture, or again birds may simply get pleasure from sunbathing. They certainly have favourite places for it, like a sheltered doorstep or roof.

Dust-bathing is a speciality of sparrows, although going from the mundane to the spectacular, it is also indulged in by the elegant hoopoe. The dustbath of fine sand or earth is scuffed up into the plumage and then shaken and preened off again. It is nothing like as common-place as water-bathing, and may be another method of dealing with parasites.

'Anting' is the oddest form of bathing. Birds like starlings and thrushes cause ants to squirt formic acid onto their plumage. There are two distinct techniques. One is to pick up an ant in the bill and hold it against the feathers, urging it to use its defence weaponry by squirting; the other is simply to get in the way of the ants and allow them to swarm all over the bird's body angrily squirting in protest. The actions

Starling 'anting'

Jay 'anting'; the wing is extended to touch the ground as an invitation ramp for ants (*Jane Burton/Bruce Coleman Ltd*)

involved in both cases are those of normal preening movements. Jays have a slight variation, where they extend their wing tips and 'shudder' them on the ground, making a ramp for the ants to climb on.

This behaviour is probably connected with the process of feather maintenance and parasite control. There must be some chemical interaction between ant-acid and the feathers: formic acid is insecticidal, so it must be bad news for feather mites and bugs. Anting is directed specially to the ends of the wing feathers. In preening these brush against the head, and a bird's head is particularly lousy, so perhaps there is a special incentive to dress it with formic acid.

Feathers are nothing less than an engineering marvel, and they have much to do with the bird success story. Given the power of flight, an animal may more easily escape enemies and take advantage of the benefits of long-distance migration to seek fresh food sources. Feathers also keep rain from the body, and they insulate a pocket of air against the skin, making it possible to control body temperature. But they wear out, and need periodic replacement, and this shedding and renewal of plumage is timed to suit the life style of each species. Clearly a migratory species needs to have its plumage in tiptop condition for long journeys. Some birds, shelducks for instance, have a flightless period when they moult all their primary feathers simultaneously, and are restricted to swimming and walking for some weeks while new ones grow. At this time they tend to congregate in large numbers in remote places where they are least disturbed. But most of our garden birds, moulting two or three times a year, tend to lose a few feathers, from both sides at a time, so that although they are working at reduced efficiency for a while, they do have warmth and flight capability all the time.

Brightly coloured and patterned, feathers are used at courting time to dazzle potential partners or intimidate rivals. A song bird will look markedly different before and after the nesting season: having fed one or two clutches of hungry juveniles, it may well look the worse for wear, so the moult is a welcome chance of a new suit of clothes. Food deficiencies may sometimes affect plumage, especially round the head where there may be a few bare patches. This will be a signal for you to increase the allowance of B complex vitamins on the birdtable: give a little bit of cheese!

The most common feather abnormality is albinism, where a bird has white or part white plumage. A true albino has no colour pigment at all, but in most cases the colouring is patchy. Urban life, with a high proportion of 'artificial' birdtable food, is a contributory factor. In a survey of albinism, it was found that the six most commonly affected species were blackbird, house sparrow, starling, swallow, rook and jackdaw. The condition may vary from moult to moult with the individual concerned, it may increase or decrease, or an albino may suddenly transform into normal plumage.

Albinism is known in mammals. Grey squirrels show it occasionally, red squirrels rarely, hedgehogs often enough, as well as badgers. It doesn't seem to be much of a disadvantage to the individual concerned, but it must make him conspicuous to predators.

# 3 THE BORDER JUNGLE

If the lawn is an open stage presenting public drama, then we must look to the paths, the flower borders and the jungle interior of the shrubbery for the backstage drama. And of the life struggles and pleasures played out here, we shall only catch revealing glimpses. Lift a stone at the edge of the lawn or on a path and a whole new world comes into view. Ants, spiders and bugs scurry away into the nearest patch of darkness. They don't like the sun. They prefer the moist secret place under the protection of that stone. So put it back carefully after having a good look.

One of the creatures you are most likely to uncover is the woodlouse. This one especially will shun the warmth of the sun. He is a crustacean, closely related to the marine shrimps and lobsters. Most of the class are aquatic and the woodlouse is one of the very few to adapt, fairly successfully, to life ashore. Unlike spiders and insects he's not water-tight, and his lifestyle is heavily geared to the avoidance of desiccation.

He is very sensitive to fluctuations in temperature and humidity, and in dry conditions he quickly succumbs. So he looks for a home under a stone or behind the loose bark of a dead tree. And he is most active at night, when the air is damper.

When they moult, woodlice often appear partly white, and may be mistaken for albinos, but the shell moults off in stages and as one half loosens it simply appears white. The animal eats the moulted skin section, as it is a valuable source of chalk. (There is one white wood-louse species, which you are less likely to see because it is found only underground in ants' nests – Hoffmansegg's woodlouse.) The pill woodlouse rolls into a ball when disturbed, rather like a hedgehog. I suppose rolling up helps to protect it from small attackers, but not from robins and blackbirds, or hedgehogs for that matter. Our bantams are very pleased to be taken on a stone-lifting tour of the garden, and relish whatever woodlice are revealed. But most spiders seem reluctant to take them, one exception being a beast called *Dysdera*, a red-legged pale-yellow-bodied nocturnal spider.

I think no garden is complete without a sheet of corrugated iron carefully placed to provide a happy home for field mice and toads and

Slow worm with young; they will be grateful for a piece of corrugated iron laid in a secluded corner of the garden (*Sdeuard Bisser ôt*)

slow worms. Slow worms, especially, are very common in my area, and it is rare indeed in summer time to lift the corrugated without finding at least one. As lizards, they much enjoy basking in the sun, but like to retreat to the security of the underworld below a log or stone, or even a pile of leaves.

Another creature you will find under a stone is the garden black ant. It has to be said that he can also be found invading the house, pioneering five-lane antways across your carpets on his way to the sugar in the pantry. This is the species involved in those spectacular marriage flights. When disturbed, there is a great panic in the nest, and the workers bustle about, picking up eggs, grubs and cocoons and carrying them below to underground chambers. They live in a world of touch and smell, light just spelling trouble for them. The wingless ants are the Workers, which has to be spelt with a capital W, because they do everything. Divided into groups, there are those which forage for food; nurserymaids, caring for the eggs and larvae, regulating their warmth and humidity by moving them about the nest; workers-in-waiting to the Queen; soldiers on guard, their weapons the acid-squirting tails or their stings. On lifting a stone or piece of bark you only reveal the tip of the iceberg. Underground is a whole series of galleries and nestchambers. The colony is no passing fancy, it is a long term project, growing all the time. Occasionally there will be a palace revolution and splinter groups will break away to establish themselves elsewhere.

Ants are regarded as pests by most gardeners, and they can do harm by loosening soil around plant roots. But they are great destroyers of yet other 'pests', emerging from their nests to hunt small insects and caterpillars and to exploit aphids for their 'milk'.

Many flower borders seem to consist of a few carefully planted annuals surrounded by a desert of bare earth, and the bare earth is an abominable sight, non-productive and incredibly difficult to maintain. Plants have a powerful urge to grow, and given the warmth and light of the sun you will have a life's work trying to stop them and it is a crime against life to try. Given the sun as our primary source of energy, green plants, by virtue of the magical photosynthesis, are the only agents capable of converting this energy into food suitable for animals.

Bare patches of earth make no useful contribution at all. The striking thing about those plants we choose to call weeds is that they are fast movers, with a fierce desire to succeed, in direct contrast with the reluctance of some of those exotic introductions which decorate many gardens. It's difficult to get on top of a plant like a dandelion which may produce 12,000 fruits, each keen to keep the species going and to make its own mark. Their advantage is that they belong here, and they succeed by virtue of thousands of years of research and development which has equipped them for this particular niche, without any artificial propagation or marketing skills. Most garden activities, like weeding or pest control, seem designed to eliminate or reduce competition and it's an uphill struggle. Lie back and enjoy those dandelions.

> *Shock-headed Dandelion*
> *That drank the fire of the sun.*
>
> 'The Idle Flowers' Robert Bridges

If you can bring yourself to face the neighbours, have a nettle bed. Young fresh nettles really are good to eat, ask any caterpillar. But stir yourself to cutting portions of the bed every now and then, to keep those fresh young shoots coming right through the season. By the same token leave a few cabbages for the lovely cabbage white butterfly. Why not? What pleasure is there in a garden with no dancing butterflies?

It is not so easy to defend some other plant eaters. Slugs and snails, for instance, are most interesting animals, yet they appeal to no one. Slimy crawlers, leaving a trail of snotty mucus behind them, eating your prize plants secretly by dead of night – they can't win. Although it may seem that their principal food is young lettuces, the fact is that there are many species and they are very catholic in their tastes, mostly going for damaged or decomposing vegetable material.

Some live underground, some feed mainly on fungi and animal droppings, some climb plants. And of course their depredations are most noticeable in the spring, when relatively little new growth is replacing the autumn and winter plenty, from their point of view, of unwanted green stuff.

As for the slime, it is their protective shell. Few predators relish it, so the slug survives. But it presents a problem at mating time, solved as the two partners first line up alongside each other and then eat each other's slime, before exchanging sperm.

Slugs are snails. Both of these creatures are molluscs. But in the slug the shell is as near absent as makes no difference. In biological terms there is little distinction between them, but in human terms most people find the snail the more endearing of the two, if that isn't pitching it a bit high! Certainly the shell is a marvel of engineering, and a most beautiful form when looked at with a modicum of objectivity. While a mammal's interior skeleton is covered with muscles and soft pliable skin, insects and their like have their strengthening material on the outside, rather like a coat of armour. In molluscs like the snail, the cuticle forms this exoskeleton, a fine piece of structural engineering. Cuticle is a strong composite material rather like fibreglass, with the protein *chiton* as a fibre component. As the snail grows, so the shell grows with it; molluscs do not moult in the style of insects. But a built-in snag limits the physical size of both: as the animal becomes larger the exoskeleton gets relatively thinner, so it is vulnerable to buckling. A mammal skeleton is cushioned from shock. A snail is condemned to being snail-sized, and the giants so popular in science fiction are doomed to stay on the drawingboard.

> *And though she doth but very softly go,*
> *However 'tis not fast, nor slow, but sure;*
> *And certainly they that do travel so,*
> *The prize they do aim at, they do procure.*

'*Upon the Snail*' John Bunyan

The commonest garden snail is *Helix aspersa*, a sadly treated species for one so perfect. His colour and shape may vary from region to region, according to the character of the soil and, to a certain extent, the activities of predators. In areas where chalk is scarce his shell will be thinner. He makes his home under a stone, in a wall crevice or under a convenient plank of wood and once he has chosen it, he returns there after every foraging trip. Generations of snails will use a particularly

White-lipped banded snail *Cepaea hortensis:* good news for hedgehogs and song thrushes (*M. W. F. Tweedie*)

enticing hole, so that in the course of time they enlarge it, especially where the rock is soft such as limestone. They are hermaphrodite, each individual having both male and female sex organs, but they join together in order to exchange sperm, after an astonishing courtship ceremony in which you may actually see them approach each other and fire chalky darts into each other's skin. The egg masses of miniature ping pong balls are a common sight under stones.

It is hardly necessary to say what snails eat, but it is only fair to point out that they prefer nettles when they're given the option. And remember that snails themselves are good to eat for man and beast. It is the largest British snail, *Helix pomatia*, which is most prized for the table. A large creamy-yellow snail, commonest in chalk or limestone downland, it is known as the Roman snail since it is supposed to have been the Romans who introduced it. In fact the Romans are said to have fattened it for the table much as they prepared pigeon squabs. Anyway, this is the edible 'escargot'. However, the garden snail *aspersa* is perfectly edible and is doubtless often enough passed off as *pomatia*, in a triumph of commerce over biology.

Many other creatures eat snails, including their arch enemy the hedgehog, everybody's garden pet! But there are one or two curious techniques used by would-be consumers of meat for dealing with the problem of the shell which protects it. Glow worms, for instance, are fond of snails. They first paralyse the mollusc by injection; the meat liquifies and the insect sucks it up, leaving an empty shell. The technique of the thrush, while less horrifying, is scarcely less delicate. Choosing a suitable stone as an anvil, the thrush hops into the flower border to find a specimen of *Cepaea* the exotically banded and colour-camouflaged hedge snail, carries the victim to the anvil and smashes the shell into several pieces. Probably it will then wipe the slime off the body, as it does with a slug, before eating it. Now the interesting thing about this activity is that though the snail exists in a whole variety of colour and banding patterns, an individual thrush tends to select one particular version of the snail. Once it has 'got its eye in' on, say, a pink snail with four black bands, that is the one it invariably goes for. You can confirm this by examining the broken shell pieces around the anvil. (Beware of an anvil used by more than one thrush!) So the thrush acts as an evolutionary agent, encouraging the snail to produce a whole range of cryptic colourations.

Why is the song thrush the only British bird that does this? There is no structural adaptation – no anatomical suitability – which gives the thrush an edge over other birds and fits him specially for it. Opportunist blackbirds often steal snails from thrushes – indeed they have learnt to listen for the sound of the thrush hammering snails on the anvil, so that they may hasten to enjoy the reward without doing any of the work. But the nearest a blackbird has been seen to engage in snail-bashing for itself is when it has shaken the snail vigorously in a variation of the beak-wiping movement. So we must be left with admiration for the two song thrushes which were once seen to deal with 29 snails in less than 8 hours.

The flower border has many examples of these curious predator/prey relationships. The inoffensive-looking ladybird may not look a carnivore, but a meat-eating predator he is. Not exactly the cunning fox or the swift sparrowhawk of the insect world, he ambles quietly up to take advantage of the greenfly which never consider the possibility of running away. So cosy is the relationship that the ladybird beetle lays its eggs conveniently close to a colony of greenfly aphids; when the larvae emerge, the dining room is close by, and they can munch at leisure. And when they are grown into the full brightly coloured glory of adult ladybirds they have the security of being thoroughly distasteful themselves, so that they are relatively immune from attack. Those bright reds and blacks serve as a warning to all comers that they are unpalatable. Other, less fortunate, insects must protect themselves by camouflage colouring, or by venturing out only at night, or by living underground.

Ladybirds aren't the only aphid-botherers. Blue tits will eat them, hover-flies and lacewings will eat them, in enormous quantities. But there are enormous quantities to be eaten as the aphids multiply at a rate which makes rabbits look like reluctant beginners. The eggs are laid at the beginning of winter to hatch in March, promptly setting about the task of producing living young which hatch from eggs incubated inside the parent body. These young mature in ten days and produce more young. These can fly and settle on herbaceous plants to feed and produce more offspring. The generations are flightless and winged alternately, and each flying generation takes itself off to pioneer the technique elsewhere. Each female greenfly produces several off-spring every day during her short life, and a single one may be res-ponsible for over 1,300 descendants in a fortnight. It is just as well that the blue tits and hover-flies are waiting in the wings.

There are many different species of aphid. Some of them – sap-suckers – pierce the tissues of plant shoots and suck with a tube-like mouth. Under a bad infestation the leaves and shoots of the plant may become distorted, in extreme cases killed. Some, like the blackfly, attack broad beans and some, like the rose-greenfly, attack roses, a crime for which they suffer heavily to the benefit of the chemical industry's bank balance.

Extracting sustenance from the sap-cells of the rose plant produces a waste product of sugar and water which is excreted by the aphids. This is keenly enjoyed by other bugs, which encourage the good work. The garden ant, for instance, will perambulate among the aphids, stroking their abdomens with antennae to stimulate the sweet secretion.

Then they take the sugar water back to the underground nest for the ant larvae to enjoy.

Aphids are subject to occasional migratory urges, when they abandon roses for grasses or some other food plant. But there are other creatures with business to do on the rose, which in all conscience has to be a good thing, since of all garden plants the rose is just about the most unproductive of useful food for other garden-livers, as opposed to garden-lovers! The leafcutter bee has a preference for rose leaves when she is looking for nest-lining material. No reasonable gardener should object, since she only takes neat circular pieces from the leaves in order to fashion them, by rolling, into egg cells which she hides away in a nest burrow in wood somewhere.

The other phenomenon which often graces roses is the frothy white mass of 'cuckoo-spit' which protects the nymph of the common frog-hopper – the little bug which jumps so smartly when you touch it gently on its behind. I hardly dare to mention it as people have such a protective pair bond with their roses, but if you persevere and produce a flourishing rosebed, in some areas you just might be lucky enough to be visited by roe deer, which enjoy them very much indeed.

Cultivated roses are impoverished plants from the point of view of animals, providing a minimum of useful food as happens when man starts to improve and beautify nature for his own, highly suspect, motives. To my way of thinking, a wild rose is a joy and most garden roses are bloated monstrosities.

Flowerheads are colourful and attractive and scented for a most important biological reason – survival. So when nurserymen monkey about with flower shapes and colours simply for the sake of man's visual satisfaction, they are playing rather horrid games. The beauty of flowers was not evolved in order to grace the polished dining-room table but to assist in the process of renewal, by attracting pollinators.

Red or crimson seem to be the most favoured colours, and shininess enhances the attraction. Perhaps the contrast with green leaves has something to do with it too. And though the object of the colour is to attract the birds and the bees, there has to be something more than beauty as a reward for pollinators: nectar. The concentration of sugar in nectar is low, about five per cent, but honey bees, for instance, are

The bumble bee's lower lip has a special extension which helps it to reach nectar (*Sdeuard Bisser ôt*)

selective enough to home in on those flowers with the mostest. Bees are the classic examples of pollinators, although many other insects like nectar. Bees smell the flower scent and see the vivid colours and patterns as well as we can, but additionally they are sensitive to ultra-violet light rays; some flowers radiate these to attract them. The bee has a specially long 'tongue', an extension of the lower lip, which helps it to suck the nectar. So the bee and the flower have a mutually beneficial arrangement, nectar for the bee in return for its services in distributing some of the pollen. Most flowers bloom simply for the purpose of attracting insects, and some seem more spectacularly successful to us than others. *Buddleia*, for instance, that exotic import from the far east, seems to have a magnetic attraction for butterflies. The generous flowerheads must be rich with sweetness, providing ecstacy for tortoiseshells, peacocks and tiger moths.

Flowerheads attract pollinators, and in due course the fertilised fruits serve a similar purpose in attracting animals which help to disseminate the seeds. *Berberis* and *Cotoneaster*, for instance, are attractive to butterflies when they flower, then in turn the birds come to take the berries. For both birds and mammals plants serve as a vital source of food, and the animals serve the plant as well when it needs help. The juicy cherry is eaten by the blackbird which may be many yards away by the time it passes the pip, coated in rich fertiliser, on to the ground. Birds are prime agents in the process of colonisation by plants. Finches shake and scatter seeds around, a just proportion falling unheeded to the ground where they have a fighting chance of surviving the winter unseen, to germinate in the spring. Maybe the finch only throws the seed a few inches, but that's enough for it to make a fresh start away from the parent plant. Seeds may, of course, travel great distances, in the stomach of a pigeon for instance, before being voided in a completely new territory, there to take their chance of breaking new ground, or being eaten by a mouse.

Jays will carry acorns hundreds of yards and bury them a few inches down as a winter store. Not all of them get found again so there's a chance for a new oak tree. Foxes will eat windfall plums and rowan berries and deposit the stones, again suitably coated with dung, a long way away. The chances for any particular seed are slim, but then consider the seed output of a plant: if every acorn became an oak tree, there would be no room on the planet for the rest of us. The rule is 'One for the rook, one for the crow, one for to rot and one for to grow'.

Not all seeds are distributed by straightforward eating and subsequent voiding. When a sparrowhawk makes a kill and dismembers a small bird, he discloses the contents of a gizzard, and there's yet another chance for a sample of corn or thistle to root. Some seeds are barbed; thistle burrs attach themselves to the coat of a passing fox or a man and take their chance of being deposited somewhere sympathetic. The wind acts as a dispersal agent in carrying dandelion parachutes and sycamore whirlers away from home and on to pastures new. Pollination is rampant on a windy day in a grass field, as any hay fever sufferer will know.

In visiting flowers, insects put themselves at risk from birds and indeed from other predatory insects. As they travel between the flowerheads they run the gauntlet of the spider traps. Spiders catch insects with a whole range of techniques: setting sticky snare-webs of orb, purse, triangular or hammock shape or open trellis work; or jumping, ambushing and chasing without the use of a web at all. The web spiders live in a world of silk and vibrations, the hunting spiders in a world of sight and touch.

The most common garden spider is the garden cross, the large beast with the striking white cross on its abdomen. It makes its web soon after dark, when you can watch it perform very easily with the discreet use of a torch. The main frame is a permanent structure, but every night it erects new radial threads, then spirals outwards from the centre. With a stable structure complete, it spins a second spiralling, this time using a different silk, gum coated. The spinning is done with the spinnerets, three pairs of appendages on the abdomen. Rather like fingers, at their tips are dozens of minute spinning tubes which extrude fluid silk which hardens on contact with air. Different internal glands produce different qualities of silk – main grid, radii, spiral and sticky spiral.

> '*Will you walk into my parlour?*' *said a spider to a fly:*
>
> '*The Spider and the Fly*' Mary Howitt

When an insect is stuck fast, its struggles transmit vibrations along the 'telegraph cable' to the spider safely hidden under a leaf. The spider then emerges to use the senses of sight and smell to evaluate the position. (If a leaf has blown into the trap by mistake, the spider cuts it out and releases it.) A suitable insect is bitten and injected with poison, then wrapped in a silken shroud drawn from the spinnerets by the hind legs. If the insect is big or difficult to handle, it may be made immobile by binding with silk before the injection. In order to suck the goodness from the prey the spider injects it with fluid which liquefies the tissues, for its small mouth cannot deal with solid food. It can go for a long time without eating, but needs water, which is why you so often find house spiders in the basin or the bath.

In the late autumn the garden cross spider spins a cocoon of yellow silk in which she lays several hundred eggs. Hidden under bark or an overlap plank on an outhouse or somewhere similar, they will sit out the winter to hatch in spring.

Why are we all so frightened of spiders? Because they are hairy, and because they have long skinny legs and fast unpredictable movements. They live secret lives in dark crannies, trap their prey by unsportsman-like methods and eat them in bizarre circumstances. On top of all that, some of them can bite (with their legs, they have no jaws) and are mildly poisonous. But have you ever been bitten? Have you ever met anyone who has been bitten?

Like all predators, spiders are themselves sought by many hungry eyes. Toads like them, and so do hunting wasps. And birds are death to spiders. Wrens, especially, birds of the hedgeways and crannies, are great spider gatherers.

The leaf litter which collects under hedgebanks and shrubberies is a prime hunting ground for birds. The sun cannot penetrate underneath and it is a home for snails and slugs, woodlice, many insects and spiders. This sort of scrub country is very good for birds, and without it you'll never achieve a high population density. This is where you will hear the blackbird shuffling about, sorting through the debris, making an astonishing volume of noise. And the dunnock will be here, too; typically a hedge bird it is unfortunately often called a hedge sparrow. Brown it may be, but with its thin beak and plump build it's no sparrow, in form or behaviour. An unobtrusive bird, it maintains a low profile in the garden, overlooked and undervalued. It likes a bit of jungle, and has flourished in the garden habitat. Weed seeds in winter, insects in summer, and the birdtable when it gets the opportunity – that's the life of the dunnock, and many other birds too. It's the diversity of food offered by a mature garden which induces so many birds either to make a permanent home in the garden, or to return year after year as summer visitors. The availability of nest-sites is important, of course, but far and away the greatest attraction is a food supply that will make it possible to rear youngsters. This is why birds rarely have the temerity to nest in the winter; it can happen, but the odds against success are high and the evolutionary process soon stops it. Birds born during a food shortage do not survive to perpetuate the mistake. Natural selection determines the breeding season, as everything else. In spring and summer there is more plant material, more insect life, more warmth, more light and longer days, so that is when the courtship comes to a climax. Small birds lays eggs in time for the nestlings to benefit from the peak caterpillar population of May and June. Sparrow-hawks lay a little later, so that they benefit from the peak small-bird population! Second broods are less likely to succeed because they have missed the insect peak. Pigeons breed almost through the year, but that is because they feed their young on milk which they can manu-facture from whatever foods are available at the time.

Choosing the building site will be part of the courtship activity, and may be decided long before construction work begins. Resident birds may have spent the winter searching for a plot, but summer visitors have less time to waste. They may select a site and begin construction on the same day. Either way the hole-nesters like tits have a more difficult task, as suitable holes are not easy to find, even if they do grow on trees! Even so, a cock great tit may find several sites and take his hen on a tour of inspection. She makes the final choice, displaying her pleasure with shivering wing movements. A particular site may be attractive to more than one pair of birds. Blue tits may build a nest and lay eggs, only to be evicted by tree sparrows which actually build

Starling with grass

another nest on top of the existing one, eggs and all, and proceed to lay their own clutch.

Building materials, as in all the most harmonious houses, will be found nearby, and will depend on the local vegetation and on the secondhand market. It is in the early stages of nest building that you have your best chance of identifying the site, because you will see birds struggling to get airborne with sticks and grass, before flying to the works. Much material may be wasted as the main timbers fall to the ground, to be left there while the bird goes off to find more. But once the framework is stable the bird will shape the cup by moving around, both ways, and working with its breast and feet. Grasses and mosses will be packed tight, and its bill will be used to work in odd strands. After the main structure is finished, another layer may be added; for instance, a blackbird will have a mud layer. Swallows and house martins also need mud, so in a dry spell remember to throw a pail of water on some bare earth for them – mud-pie making is hard work without water.

Then comes the inner lining of soft stuff like feathers. This is the stage at which birds will be grateful for any offerings you may put out for them. Things like the dog's hair combings, feathers and scraps of material (but not lengths of cotton which might get into a leg tangle). Long-tailed tits will be especially grateful for feathers, as they use prodigious quantities for nest lining. Hair of all kinds is much prized; badger hairs have been picked from barbed wire fences and pony hairs from the back of the animal. Goldfinches use the silken thread from spider's webs as a binding material when they are fastening the twig structure and to bind the wood and grasses and dandelion fluff which makes the inner lining. A goldcrest even got itself trapped and tangled in the sticky web of a garden spider, but it flew away safely when a birdwatcher rescued it.

Tie-on plant labels are a favourite nest material, though goldfinches actually untie the string, which involves quite intricate manipulative behaviour. One jackdaw's nest held 67 plant labels. Polystyrene chippings are popular, perhaps providing extra warmth and insulation – 1,500 were solemnly counted in the nest of one long-tailed tit. Pigeons go for sterner stuff, like stainless-steel wire. Short lengths of wire are not so very different from twigs, so there is really no behavioural significance in any of these odd uses of man-made materials. Birds just have nothing to learn from us in the field of low-impact technology; they use available resources to the best advantage.

Birds may build several nests. One mistle thrush actually started five, but finished two. The problem was that it was building on top of a pillar at a nuclear power station, and there wasn't just one pillar but dozens and dozens of them, regularly spaced 20 feet apart in a rectangular block. The unfortunate bird became disorientated by the multiplicity of identical sites, and didn't always land on the same pillar.

Nest building is part of a routine, and it has to start at the beginning, with the establishment of a territory and with courtship. Without this stimulus, an unmated hen is very unlikely to build a nest and lay eggs, although it does happen. (The domesticated chicken, is an example, but this is a bird which has been painstakingly selected for just this function.) Cock wrens build nests for a pastime, and in other countries the cock weaver birds build half a nest from which to display. But normally first things come first, and there's no nest without a partnership.

Birds are easily disturbed and may abandon the project in the early stages of nest building. Many desert if they are fussed, so on the whole it is best to leave them alone altogether. If you must go and look, do it in an ordinary, everyday sort of manner. Walk quietly up to the nest, talking as you go, and generally act like the blundering mammal that you are. At all costs avoid a slow approach with a direct gazing stare. The birds will resent this abnormal and inexplicable behaviour. Do not poke a finger into a hole-nest. Wrens, for instance, sit very tight, but will readily desert if you start touching them. Do not cut away leaves or twigs to see the nest more easily; this will simply be an invitation to the nearest predator. Photographers are the greatest menace in this respect. For my part I do not search for nests and I prefer to leave birds to get on with the job without my interference, and that goes as far as not getting in the way when magpies are at their dirty work of egg-thieving, or woodpeckers are baby-snatching. If a bird deserts the nest, it has to start again elsewhere from the beginning. It takes an intelligent mammal, like a fox or you or me, to have the sense to pick up the juveniles and carry them off elsewhere to start a new life!

Most small birds lay one egg a day, usually in the early morning, and start incubating as soon as the clutch is complete. But some, swifts and birds of prey like owls, for instance, lay on alternate days, or even at three-day intervals, but start incubating as soon as the first egg is laid. Thus their brood of nestlings always has a youngest – and therefore a weakest – individual. If times are hard and food is scarce, the youngest is the one to die, leaving more food and more hope for the older chicks.

Not all nests receive their complement of eggs. A cock wren will build a whole series of trial nests in the early spring. Made of moss, grasses and leaves, they will be cunningly woven into a bundle of twigs, an old coat hanging in the shed, or a creeper-clad wall. One year we had an occupied wren's nest in a coil of rope hanging in our boatstore. When the cock has successfully attracted a mate, she inspects the trial offerings and makes the final choice, finishing the job by lining the shell with feathers, then laying and incubating. But the cock still continues building nest shells and advertising for another hen, who in turn finishes a chosen nest. So the cock wren, unusually among birds, is a bigamist, with perhaps as many as three wives at once. Not surprisingly, he hardly bothers to feed the young birds, but he may condescend to conduct parties of adolescents around the neighbourhood, teaching them the hunting trade.

Some birds lay an astonishing number of eggs. I have a record of tame robins which, having laid two eggs on a garage shelf, deserted them to build another nest a couple of feet away and lay four eggs in it, which were successfully hatched and the nestlings fledged. Then the adults went back to the first nest, laying four more eggs and successfully rearing four more young. And after all that they returned yet again to nest number two and sat on four more eggs. But it is all part and parcel of the rather casual business of egg production. Among mammals, the burden of carrying the foetus for months on end and then having the responsibility of a helpless infant encourages a more sober approach to the whole process!

While on the nest, a hen robin will be fed by the cock, thus continuing a process which started in courtship, when she begged food from him as part of the ritual. Now the behaviour pays dividends as it allows her to spend more time on the nest.

Clutch sizes vary a great deal. First time breeders lay fewer eggs than they will do in later, more experienced, years. Farmland and woodland pairs lay more eggs than garden pairs because the feeding is better. In cold weather or a drought, there will be fewer eggs. Conditions may well improve between laying and hatching, but the birds have no way of foretelling this. Most of the tales which relate weather prospects to the actions of animals are so much nonsense. Unpopular though it may be to say it, meteorologists are the best weather forecasters in the animal kingdom!

As already mentioned, sparrowhawks nest late so that their young get the benefit of the peak period of small-bird availability. Another bird which arrives late is the cuckoo, usually in the third week of April, when small birds have already prepared nests and laid eggs and are all set to incubate on the hen cuckoo's behalf. And of course if you discover a nest of eggs with a single maverick, then it belongs to a cuckoo. Many other summer visitors, like the chiffchaff, arrive earlier and are earlier announcers of spring than the cuckoo, but in poetic terms he is the greatest. The male actually cuckoos, while the hen makes a bubbling noise. Cuckoos may superficially be mistaken for a sparrowhawk, but they have none of the flashpast and bezazz of the hawk. The hen drops a single egg in each chosen foster-home, and in due course the young cuckoo ejects the eggs or young of the rightful occupants, usually dunnocks or robins, using its strong back specially constructed for the purpose.

Most garden-bird eggs take some twelve to fourteen days to hatch. The parent removes the broken eggshell, and starts the hard job of feeding those ever-open mouths. The most demanding and vigorous nestling will get the lion's share of the food, so that once again there tends to be a built-in survivor if the going gets rough.

Some young birds, like plovers and ducks, leave the nest a few days after hatching; if you have a herring gull nesting on your roof, its juveniles will soon be exploring the gutters and ridges. But most small birds stay in the nest, which now becomes their nursery. Straight away the problem of sanitation arises, for as fast as food goes in one end, faeces appear at the other. But all is carefully ordered, as the droppings are elegantly encapsulated in a little gelatinous sac, and the parents carry the offering away in their beaks, dropping it at a discreet distance on to your lawn, where it should be a welcome source of nutrient.

When the young birds fledge they leave the nest for trial flights, doing their circuits and bumps and familiarising themselves with the landscape and its possibilities. On the lawn they will follow their foraging parents, begging for food with open beaks and fluttering wings. It is a hectic time for parents, and sometimes a house sparrow, say, may find itself feeding a young blackbird by mistake. The adult, carrying a juicy morsel, is stimulated by the sight of the juvenile's open gape. At this stage, in summer, the garden border will harbour many young birds which sit motionless, but flutter their wings and gape at you when you approach. Do not be misled into thinking that they have fallen out of a nest and are lost and hungry. It is a normal part of the process and they are not lost; the parent is busy looking for food and will find the baby very quickly with an interchange of calls. If you go away they will get on with it.

Not all the nests which decorate your garden belong to birds. If you have trees, or if you adjoin a park or cemetery or some such place with a fair sprinkling of trees, you will have squirrels, and they build their substantial dreys in trees. Like birds, they choose to live near you mainly because of the available food, but obviously they must have a suitable nest-site.

Red squirrels are the most popular with their long bushy tails and conspicuous ear tufts, but they are much less widespread than the ubiquitous grey. With a marked preference for conifer woods, red squirrels are subject to population fluctuations which result in periodic scarcity, so you are lucky if you have them. Just precisely what is the factor which favours the grey squirrel is not clear, but it is true that in the long term the red does not do well in areas where the grey species is abundant. Red squirrels do not fight with the greys, any more than they do amongst themselves. The red squirrel was already declining in numbers before the grey was so ill-advisedly introduced, back at the end of the nineteenth century. It was in London and at Woburn Abbey that the first grey squirrels, imported from North America, were released and in no time at all this adaptable opportunist was well established. At first he was regarded entirely as a charmer, but it was

A doubtfully welcome visitor to the birdtable—the grey squirrel (*Gwen Thompson*)

not long before his bad habits upset the foresters. Eating new shoots and ring-barking trees, the grey squirrel quickly became a pest, and the law now requires us all to exterminate them. Easier said than done, especially as many people still positively welcome him to the garden and the birdtable. Quite apart from his tree damaging activities, grey squirrels have a well-developed taste for eggs, young birds and young green shoots of all kinds, not to mention peanuts. A pity that there is no known way of making life easier for the red squirrel in our gardens, but the Forestry Commission is doing sterling work, as many of their plantations provide very favourable conditions for them.

The red squirrel drey is a compact and substantial ball of twigs and bark, lined with grasses and leaves, placed where a branch joins the main trunk of a tree. The grey's drey is rather more domed, and may be out from the trunk, placed in a large fork. Like birds the squirrel will make use of whatever convenient materials are on offer: news-paper is a common ingredient, but they have been known to use balls of string, rags, children's gloves, pencil stubs and paper bags.

Grey squirrels will eat almost anything. The red is particularly fond of pine cones, which it will collect off the ground and take to a safe branch where it eats away at the seeds, flicking the scales away until the finished cone is thrown away looking rather like an apple core.

Many birds nest in the comparative safety of a tree. Like the squirrel, rooks and herons nest out in the open for all to see, protected by the safety of numbers and the difficulty of access. Other birds take advantage of the crevices and holes found in trees which are past their prime and where old branches have rotted and fallen away, leaving an open invitation to a decaying interior. Great spotted woodpeckers, favourite garden birds, mostly operate on dead or decaying branches, looking for both insects and for nest-sites. They may damage a sound tree by barking it in order to enjoy the exuding sap (they are called sapsuckers in the United States) so they can be a nuisance to foresters, since the bark peeling opens the way to secondary infections by insects or fungi. Pines, oaks and limes are particular targets. But in the garden they can only be welcome. They have powerful chisel-tipped bills, and they use them to great effect in excavating tree-holes. They may even bore holes in telegraph posts, or in the cedar shingles of your house, all in the cause of foraging for insects! And if they find a brazil nut on the birdtable at Christmas they will take it to a tree and wedge it into a crack before splitting it with that multi-purpose tool of a beak. A nuthatch will do the same, and indeed will take over a woodpecker's nest and convert it to his requirements, reducing the entrance to a more suitable nuthatch size by plastering it with mud or clay. With its noisy

Nuthatch

liquid whistle, the nuthatch is a welcome garden visitor in the south of England, preferring mature gardens with well-grown oaks, beeches, limes and chestnuts.

Wood pigeons are common garden tree-nesters these days. Originally a woodland species, over the last hundred years they have increased enormously in numbers and are now regarded much more as farm pests and city and suburban dwellers. Curiously shy in the country yet tame in the city, the wood pigeon is even less scary than the street pigeon. A sociable bird but fiercely territorial in the breeding season, it defends its own nest-tree against all comers. On the other hand collared doves like to nest sociably, with a preference for a stand of conifers in the corner of a park or mature well-treed garden. Collared doves are now common garden birds, well established all over the country since their explosive arrival in 1955, after a rapid spread across Europe from India. Like wood pigeons, they have been known to use wire netting to reinforce their nests. Not a menace to green vegetables, they have a great love of corn or grass seed, so watch out when you are seeding the lawn.

Tits are typically tree-nesters, and that accounts for their readiness to adopt nestboxes, which so far as they are concerned are an acceptable substitute for a conveniently decayed tree trunk with an entrance hole. They spend such time hunting insects in trees, so obviously it is convenient to nest nearby. In woodland, where caterpillars are plentiful, they lay an average of eleven eggs, whereas in city gardens the average is down to nine; the fact is that although they do well on birdtable food in winter, they are at a disadvantage in summer when they need protein-rich insect food to raise young. They do take greenfly from rose bushes, but these are a poor substitute for caterpillars, and a pair of blue tits may bring an average of 700 caterpillars a day to their nestlings. They also take other insects, and are very fond of honey bees.

Honey bees also nest in tree holes, and blue tits will deliberately hang about the hive entrance (and this applies to the man-made beehive as well) picking off the odd bee. In fact in some parts of the country they are actually known as bee birds, along with the whitethroat and the spotted flycatcher, both keen bee-fanciers. Both bees and wasps are good to eat, except for the sting of course, and the tits know the difference between the male (stingless) bee and the female stingers, and deal with them accordingly. Blue tits may appear to be little charmers, but just see one perching on a branch, holding a bee in one foot and picking at it like a hawk. It is a ferocious little animal. It deals with the venom by beating the bee against the perch, and by rubbing the insect to squeeze out the poison and discard the sting. On a cold day, when bees are torpid, the tits may actually enter the hive to go hunting. They are fond of honey too. Put some on the birdtable and you will find it is welcome to tits and also to blackbirds and woodpeckers.

Before sugar, honey was man's only sweetening substance, of course, and it is an excellent source of instant energy: one spoonful represents the distillation of nectar from visits to 50,000 flowers. Having found a good source of nectar, the foraging bee returns to the hive and conveys the information to the other bees by dancing. Using the sun as a reference point, his waggle-dance communicates 'bearing and distance-off' and the degree of attractiveness.

A honey-bee swarm may contain as many as 50,000 individuals at the height of summer. The bee/man relationship is long established, maybe 10,000 years old, with the bee making honey and us providing a welcome and a house. Bees are principal pollinators of apples and many fruitgrowers hire occupied beehives in order to ensure maximum pollination in their orchards. Apart from that, and our share of the honey, we benefit from the beeswax, used in the manufacture of things like candles and furniture polish.

Many birds search the foliage and bark of trees for insects and caterpillars; treecreepers, for instance, make a speciality of searching in and around the bark for bugs of all kinds, insect eggs and larvae. They go for gall wasps too, the insects responsible for some of those curious marble-like growths on leaves and twigs. Woodpeckers attack and split open galls in the search for the insects inside them. There are more than 1,000 different plant galls in Britain, caused by the activities sometimes of insects and sometimes of a fungus. They are vegetable growths, typically found on oaks and willows as an abnormality of the plant. There are many shapes and forms, some found on the roots, some on twigs and leaves and some on flowers, all providing a home and nourishment for the larvae of the insect which stimulated them.

78

Sometimes the original inhabitant is himself parasitized by another species which takes over the gall, and this parasite may itself be hyper-parasitised by yet another intruder. So the gall may become host to a mixed community!

> He walks still upright from the root,
> Meas'ring the timber with his foot;
> And all the way, to keep it clean,
> Doth from the bark the wood-moths glean,
> He, with his beak, examines well
> Which fit to stand and which to fell.

'*The Woodpecker*' Andrew Marvell

The familiar oak-apple, growing in the month of May, is caused by a gall-wasp, *Biorhiza pallida*. There are several chambers inside, each with a wasp larvae which eats its way out into the world in July, leaving a neat hole to mark its exit. Another oak gall resembles a composition marble, growing this time on a leaf and caused by the gall-wasp

Great spotted woodpecker and galls

79

*Andricus kollari*. Waxy pale-green in summer, this one turns reddish-brown in October.

The typical willow gall is that of the beangall sawfly, which produces colours ranging through red, yellow and green. Gall insects, wasps, midges, sawflies and aphids, travel from soil to leaves or twigs in their life cycle, stimulating the gall in which they deposit eggs which become larvae, emerging to migrate down to pupate in the soil. And on the migration they are preyed upon by birds like the treecreeper and woodpecker.

With so much preying and being preyed upon, it sometimes seems a marvel that anything manages to survive to breed. Roughly speaking a creature's lifespan is related to its size. Greenfly have short lives filled with child-bearing, swans may last as long as a man with a modest quantity of leisure activity thrown in. Most animals have a potential lifespan far in excess of their actual length of life. Most birds die in the first flush of youth. The period of greatest danger is just after they leave the nest. An average eight-week-old blackbird, for example, has an expectation of eighteen months. Forty per cent of the adults die each year, and less than ten per cent of those leaving the nest will reach the age of five.

The peak mortality is in May and June, so what do they die of? Cats, predators, pesticides, chemicals, starvation, injury and car accidents. Not from parasites, for though birds are not short of these passengers, part of the bargain between a parasite and its host is that it is not in the parasite's interest to kill him. They have a working agreement! Probably most animals die unseen, for if they are injured or sick they tend to hide away in solitary misery. And it is in the nature of things that if they are in a weakened condition they will not stay that way long: either they recover quickly, or something will turn up to give them a quick end. If you find an animal which allows you to go close enough to touch it or pick it up, you can be virtually certain that it has not long to live.

> *Their little corpse the robin redbreast found,*
> *And strew'd with pious bill the leaves around.*

John Gay

A dying tree provides a sympathetic home for many other plants and animals, including woodlice, which like the damp dark space behind the peeling bark. But crows like woodlice (*Joe B. Blossom*)

But when you do see a dead body, at least it will tell you what animals are about. Dead foxes, hedgehogs, rats, grass snakes and slow worms on the roads, for instance, may sometimes be the first indication that these species are presen . And if there are dead hedgehogs on the roads there's not much doubt that they are survived by live ones. Of course, we must recognise that a steady supply of dead and dying animals is good news for carrion-eaters, like foxes, badgers and crows. And on a smaller scale, there are many beetles which live by courtesy of the dead, using one of their two techniques. Beetles like the sexton beetle gather at the body of, say, a mouse or bird and scrape away the soil to bury it, or pull it to a burying place. Their motive is to lay eggs alongside, providing a ready food supply for the young grubs which take up residence in the body as they consume it. Then there are carrion beetles which don't bother to bury the body, but simply eat it and lay eggs by it. All rather ghoulish, but these beetles are most valuable in tidying up.

Trees die, in their own good time, and in doing so they provide rich pickings for many other plants and animals for many years. One of the pathetic sadnesses in public parks is the passion of the authorities for tidying away a tree the moment it looks as if it is going to topple. Shortening the death throes by cutting up and burning the rotten timber denies life to a whole community of animals. A fallen tree becomes a fairyland of coloured mosses, lichens, ferns and fungi, and provides rich hunting for treecreepers, woodpeckers and many other birds. With a few holes bored in the trunk, it may be heaven for solitary bees and wasps, so persuade the authorities to allow a few trees to die gracefully. If they are in a dangerous state then cut them down, but leave them where they lie to provide an adventure playground for children as well as badgers.

Dead trees may be a forester's nightmare, but for a garden-naturalist the best thing of all is for a tree to die of old age, perhaps hastened by wood-boring beetles and a fungus which sucks the life out of it. This is as it should be, for a garden without dead wood is impoverished. A vast community of plants, fungi and animals live on dead wood and help with the rotting process of recycling. Death and decay are a necessary and healthy part of life. Especially is that true in a forest, for where a tree topples, the leafy canopy is broken and a pool of sunlight penetrates the floor. The light stimulates saplings to grow and race each other towards the sky where daylight is unlimited. In time the open wound in the canopy is healed. Again, it is the sunlight which makes the whole system work. Every blade of grass and every leaf is a chemical factory soaking up sunlight and ultimately providing energy-rich substances from which flowers, fruits and timber are made. Nutrients in dead timber and leaves are essential to the continuing story.

> *They took all the trees*
> *And put them in a tree museum*
> *And they charged all the people*
> *A dollar and a half just to see 'em*
> *Don't it always seem to go*
> *That you don't know what you've got*
> *Till it's gone*

'Big Yellow Taxi' Joni Mitchell

# 4 FOUR WALLS

Four walls and a roof make a very comfortable naturalist's hideaway. All mod cons and no weather problems, you can sit comfortably by your garden window and watch to your heart's content. You may have to put up some net curtain so that you can watch undisturbed, and your neighbours may think you're a peeping tom, but that is one of the hazards of being a garden-watcher. A pair of binoculars mounted on a tripod will increase your enjoyment enormously and in this situation the weight of the glasses hardly matters, so you can take advantage of those government-surplus battleship-type glasses which are relatively cheap but heavy.

Your birdtable will be only a few feet away and will be a constant source of interest. What species of bird, mammal and insect come to visit; when do they come and how often; what do they take and what are their relationships with other visitors? Birds will take astonishing quantities of food from the birdtable, as anyone who feeds them pea-

Blue tit and peanuts

nuts *ad lib* will know. Sparrows have learnt to take stale bread to water in order to soften it and make it more palatable, a piece of behaviour pioneered by a few individuals, possibly yet to be learnt by others. Peanuts are not exactly a natural food in our gardens, so at first blue tits had to learn about them before passing the message on. There is no doubt that birds are capable of this kind of learning, and the saga of the milk-bottle tops is an excellent example of it. Here is a case where wildlife-watching from windows revealed a remarkable story. Anyone who provisions a birdtable will know that tits have a great craving for fat, often suet or bacon rinds, and their most spectacular technique for satisfying that craving is to prise off milk-bottle tops and drink the cream from your daily pinta.

It's not surprising that tits were first to exploit the free milk. They're lively, acrobatic birds, with that sense of curiosity which leads them to explore and investigate. Tits are good at intelligence tests. You've probably seen those amusing films showing them hauling up peanuts on string, hand over hand (or should I say beak over claw) and heaving oo gauge railway trucks loaded with peanuts up an inclined plane. So it's not too much to imagine one particular blue tit with an exceptionally high IQ, perching on top of a shiny white bottle and hacking his way through the cardboard top. This was first recorded in 1921, over 50 years ago, near Southampton. But other tits imitated and the habit spread through the suburbs like wildfire. Rather like gulls following the plough, parties of tits followed the milk cart, and attacked the bottles within minutes of them hitting the doorstep.

Years ago milk bottles were sealed with a waxy cardboard disc and if it wasn't too well sealed, they'd just rip it out and chuck it away. Or they'd just take out the central disc, or they'd peel off layer after layer of paper till the cap was thin enough to smash. And then the ecstasy of the cream – what a way to start the day. They'd drink as much as the top two inches, leaning further and further into the bottle; indeed, many tits have leaned too far, and drowned in a sea of milk.

Some people say that the tits go for Channel Islands milk especially and – unkindly – have tried switching foil tops, between Channel Islands and ordinary milk; but the bird sticks with the gold top, not the gold taste. Probably each bird tends to keep to the colour it first learnt to open. If you think that the birds are getting the best part of the milk by drinking the cream, remember that the really nutritious part is the milk underneath, so the blue tit is doing you a good turn by drinking off the fatty top.

When aluminium-foil tops were introduced, the dairymen thought they'd foiled the birds as well as the milk bottle. But the beak of a tit-mouse, scaled down, is as powerful as the building contractor's pneumatic drill: a few thumps, a crack, a hole, and off we go again. People have tried all sorts of ways to keep their milk intact. Everything, that is, except getting out of bed when the milkman calls. They've persuaded the milkman to cover the bottles with flat stones – one tit removed the stone three times in quick succession; or with a paint-tin lid – the bird just sat on the edge and tiped it off. They've persuaded the milkman to cover bottles with a tea cloth, an interesting one because it meant that the bird was denied the stimulus of *seeing* the milk. But they even beat that. I think the prize story is the one about the school in Surrey. One November morning the milkman delivered 300 bottles of milk. By the time the caretaker had arrived, the birds had opened 57 of them.

Only one kind of milk-bottle top foils them: the crown cork – that

Blue tits at milk bottles

heavy tinny one with a sharp crinkly edge used on sterilised milk bottles – and also beer bottles. It's a comforting thought that birds are defeated by beer bottles – anybody's Saturday night would be ruined by a band of drunken blue tits.

Of course, in behaviour terms, opening a milk bottle requires no new technique for a tit. As part of his normal daily activity he searches trees for insects and will peel away the bark as part of the search; the milk bottle pioneers were really looking for bugs. But that is not to suggest that birds do everything on an automatic, programmed basis. If you define intelligence as the capacity to learn and to adapt behaviour as a result of experience, birds definitely have it. They have some programmed responses; the essential movements of flight are innate, so that the young bird knows instinctively what he has to do. But trial and error improves the performance. Birds quickly learn to ignore noises or movements which prove to be harmless, the young learn from their parents, adults learn from each other. And the classic case is that of the tits and the milk.

It is just as well that blue tits are pretty, and have an amusing and acrobatic way of behaving, because they sometimes indulge in other bad habits, such as putty-eating and paper-tearing. They can do a lot of damage when they enter a room and start to strip the wallpaper, perching by the edge of the paper and tearing it away with sideways movements of the head. Yet again, this is probably just another version of the bark-tearing behaviour. Even when there is plenty of food on a nearby birdtable and the bird is not hungry, an urgent drive is in operation, just as with a fox which enters a chicken run and kills every single fowl; it is not because he needs to eat them or because he finds it fun, but because it is his nature and his purpose in life to pounce on and kill anything suitable *which moves*. He is unable to stop himself once the killing starts. So the blue tit continues searching for food by tearing away the wallpaper, or the putty on the window, even though he is not hungry. Having said that, though, it is also true that outbreaks of paper-tearing may be most prevalent in years when natural food is scarce and when continental tits may invade us in large numbers. Fortunately they do some good work round the house by taking the odd house-fly or spider.

To be consistent, as I often praise the usefulness of herring gulls and foxes as scavengers and carrion feeders – general tidiers-up of the environment – I ought to be in favour of house-flies, but they are carriers of foul diseases and the cause of unpleasantnesses like diarrhoea. They lay eggs in a place where they can be hatched into a world of dung and decay, on carrion and ordures on which they promptly set to and feed. I can live without them actually in the house. But spiders are different, and on the whole I like to see them around. Even those dense webs in neglected corners are rather attractive, and I try hard to like the longlegged spooky house spider that makes them. But they are all grist to the blue tit mill.

There is good feeding for small birds around the windows of a house, especially if it's a rather old house with peeling paint and slightly neglected stone or brickwork. There will be many bugs and spiders for the questing wren and tit. But sometimes birds actually fly into the windows, at best giving themselves a bruise, and at worst killing themselves. The trouble often occurs when there are windows on opposite

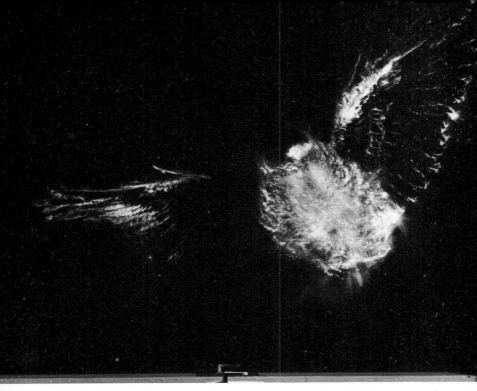

Not a bird, but the impression left on Stuart Wilton's bedroom window 24 hours after a barn owl had flown against it, at 1 am on a moonlit night, making a noise such as a tennis ball might make if thrown against the window. It seems that the barn owl must have realised at the last minute that it was in danger as its wings are in a 'braking' position and the underside of the body has taken most of the impact. There was no trace of a body below the window, so the lucky bird appears to have survived. The incident has given rise to a tentative suggestion that owls may possess a weak form of sonar, providing information leading to collision-avoidance action (*Stuart Wilton*)

walls of a room and the bird can see right through from the front to the back garden, or whatever. Then it flies through full of confidence, only to be brought up with a smart jerk when it hits the glass. Venetian blinds may be the answer or, dare I say it, dirty windows – anything to show the bird that the glass is there. On sunny days the problem may be caused by a reflection of the garden, and in this case blinds or curtains are of no use. Outside netting will serve, but is not very attractive. Cut-out shapes of sparrowhawks often work: one man who worked in a modern office block with a plethora of glass and concrete found that an average of six birds were being killed every week and stuck up a buzzard silhouette with some success. But probably any sort of pattern which breaks up the apparently empty window will do. In Denmark they sell oval glass shapes for hanging in windows, and in Switzerland they etch hawk shapes on the glass. When the Young Ornithologists Club carried out a survey on this subject, they found that the problem mainly occurred in spring and summer, when birds are busy and fledglings learning to fly. It is not confined to diurnal birds; often enough owls will fly into windows at night. If you find birds stunned under your window, the best treatment is to put them somewhere dark and very warm for an hour or so. That will often do the trick.

The actual fabric of a house provides many a happy hunting ground and homesite for animals. Try to see your home through their eyes and consider its potential for both wild plants and animals. Imagine yourself a bat or an owl and the roof cavity immediately becomes just another kind of a cave. Holes in the tiles or in the wall are just another version of a hole in a tree for a tit or a starling. The eaves represent a rocky cliff-overhang for a house martin. The walls are cliffsides for ferns, especially if there are cracks and crevices which may hold a little soil. Limestone is perhaps the most sympathetic of wall materials, but plants will get a foothold almost anywhere, given half a chance. Lichens are well suited to living on walls and roofs. They are compound plants, part fungus and part algae, with the algae growing inside the fungus and providing sun-ripened food for it to feed on. So they are a nice example of symbiosis – two different species living together to their mutual benefit.

Creeper of any kind growing on your walls will improve the wild-life possibilities enormously. That much-maligned plant ivy is the best of all, providing cover right through the year for birds and insects, nest-sites and, best of all, berries which fruit very late into the winter and provide a valuable food source at a difficult time. Ivy is a beautiful plant and is very attractive to insects in the autumn when it flowers – so in turn it has yet more attractions for birds!

In wall crevices you will find the bluish silk snare of the *Amaurobius*

Swallows at nest, comfortably indoors (*S. C. Porter/Bruce Coleman Ltd*)

spiders which lurk in the depths waiting for unwary flies to entangle themselves. Under the eaves you may be lucky enough to have a colony of house martins nesting. Originally a mountainside and cliffside bird, the house martin has learnt to colonise buildings as a substitute. Protected by the overhanging ledge of the roof, it plasters its mud nest directly on to the precipice of the wall and there it will have a running battle with the sparrows which try to take over the properties.

Wasps build under eaves, or hanging from an internal joist. At first the nest is the size of a golf ball, beautifully constructed by the queen of papier-mâché made from wood fibre. The first generation of workers is born here, fed and nurtured by the queen on a diet of chewed flies. Extension work to the building makes room for more cells and more workers, and by the time it's finished the nest is the size of a football. At the approach of autumn a generation of males and females is produced with the capacity to fly and mate. The resulting queens hibernate, to survive into the New Year to begin a new colony, while the males die when the cold weather overtakes them. The docile hornet sometimes nests in outhouses, to the panic of everyone in sight, although it is markedly reluctant to sting. It is much bigger than the common wasp, and is yellow and red instead of yellow and black. Wasps are widely regarded as a nuisance, and countless nests and queens are destroyed; yet arguably they do more good than harm. The worker wasps lead an exemplary life carrying home insect prey to feed their young, and in truth the sting never justifies the fear it rouses. Honey-bee stings are a great deal worse! Wasps nests are attacked by woodpeckers and by magpies, which rip them apart to extract the pupae and larvae. But sometimes the wasps fight back, and on occasion they will drive blue tits away from a choice bone or fruit on the birdtable.

Solitary bees and wasps make their burrow homes in wood or suitable walls, plastering the entrance with mud or clay and stocking the interior with honey and pollen, paralysed caterpillars or spiders, depending on the species involved. Mining bees burrow and make a little clay pot for the egg cell, stocking it with honey and then putting a lid on it for safety. Sometimes the nest hole will be in a window frame or a ventilation brick or a post; sometimes even a keyhole is pressed into service.

Indoors, taking advantage of the warm dry surroundings house mice will thrive, given any encouragement. They are a commensal species, living with man because it suits them. And if conditions are sympa-

The queen wasp works on the nest, while the first generation of workers is still in the larvel stage inside (*M. W. F. Tweedie*)

Common toad (*Lionel E. Day*)

thetic, with access to plenty of food, they will multiply fruitfully, with up to six litters of six young every year. The brown rat is another commensal with man, though fortunately not as prolific as the mouse.

Down in the cellar, where it is dank and dark, the common toad likes to make his home base. A domesticated, faithful and tame creature, it is a pity that he is so unattractive to us. Along with other amphibians and reptiles, he is not popular. Poor toad, he likes to make himself at home in a nest scooped under a stone or in a corner of the cellar all day, then he comes out at dusk, or after a shower. He's an excellent climber; many's the time people have suggested that it is impossible for their toad to 'escape' from the cellar, when the great fat beast clearly hasn't gone short of a meal for years. They climb so well you may even find them sitting comfortably in an abandoned bird's nest high off the ground. Long-lived and sedentary, they are slow movers, vulnerable yet protected by poison glands in the skin which make them distasteful to potential predators. They eat almost any living thing they can cram in to their mouths. Any moving prey, like a snail or a worm, is watched with a patient gaze, followed by a quick grab. Fastidiously the toad removes the soil from an earthworm as he feeds it in. Apart from the annual safari to the breeding pond, he stays at home. Try him with a wriggling worm – he'll soon become the family favourite.

Sometimes the cellar can be the venue for a most astonishing natural phenomenon that has the neighbourhood shaken. In that damp and dark world flourish moulds and mildews, yeasts and rusts. Fungi come in all shapes and sizes, and since they can extract carbohydrates direct from living or dead organic material they can manage to thrive away from the sunlight, provided there is a supply of, for instance, decaying timber. Part of their function is to assist in the process of breaking down and scavenging potential earth-cloggers. And while this is an admirable trait in the primeval forest, it may be less welcome in Acacia Avenue. The fungi reproduce from spores which germinate when temperature, humidity and habitat all conspire together to offer the right conditions. After a long period of quiet and unobtrusive growth and preparation, one day the kraken wakes. The fruit may come up practically overnight in a dramatic eruption. And if there happens to be a flagstone or concrete in the way it simply gets lifted up to allow room for the fungus to expand. Quite astonishing weights may be lifted.

Fungi find a comfortable home at the opposite end of the house, too, and indeed if conditions are right you will be only too aware of dry rot and wet rot all over the place. And along with some notorious insects like the beetle which goes by the name of woodworm, they may cause you much grief. But if all is well, your roof-space will provide dry warm quarters for yet another community. More bugs and spiders will reside here, starlings and sparrows will worm their way in through incredibly small entrance holes and import grasses to improve the facilities; maybe swallows, even barn owls if you provide a decent-sized entrance and an apple box for a nursery. Deep crevices and ledges may entice swifts to come in from their aerial outdoor life, but they tend to go for old buildings, tall towers and tall houses, anywhere where there's a dark inaccessible hole. The nest will be made of material collected in the air itself – flying straws, feathers, cotton – all gummed together with saliva. In the romantic Far East, cousins of swifts – cave swiftlets – provide the salivary secretion which spawns birdsnest soup; horrid thought. Presumably there's no reason why we shouldn't eat British swifts' birdsnest soup, the saliva must be much the same. But it is well and truly mixed with feathers and other junk and would need a lot of cleaning. By all accounts the tasteless gelatinous stuff has precious little food value anyway but in the East where it is served in soup or jelly, mixed with chicken and so on, it is supposed to have aphrodisiac qualities.

Swallows may come in to your loft, although garages and outhouses usually provide a more open access to the joists and purlins they use as a foundation for their muddy, grassy, construction. The Romans are said to have used them as homing pigeons, carrying news of chariot races by a process of colour marking. Wild birds were taken from the nest on the day of the meeting, and released to dash home to the hungry juveniles. Nowadays we use pigeons for somewhat similar purposes of message carrying and feral pigeons may well colonise your house, especially in the centres of cities where old houses have the right sorts of nooks and crannies or access to the roof-loft.

Like the house martins, street pigeons were originally wild birds of the sea cliffs, foraging for seeds along the clifftops, and they are all semi-domesticated versions of the wild rock dove. Now they claim squatter's rights in every city. Much persecuted, and with reason, by the council pest controllers, they are practically bombproof as a species. As fast as demolition works move them out of one condemned area, they colonise another. I have a soft spot for them, even though they make a filthy mess and carry every disease known to man. They have a lot of the characteristics of people, and that must be good, mustn't it? They're resilient, opportunist birds, quick to take advantage of a soft option, quick to latch on to the fact that people need friendship, very often run short of it, and that friendship with a pigeon is better than none at all. So they paddle about the streets looking for free handouts and they build their nests on the nooks and crannies of windowsills and ventilator shafts and holes in walls high above the traffic.

The well-grown squabs are very good to eat, so men used to go to the sea caves to collect them and soon realised that they could make life easier for the rock doves by cutting out suitable nest ledges – within easy reach, of course. And provided the men didn't take too many squabs, the pigeon population did well, and everyone was happy. In the course of time, men decided to save themselves the bother of going to the beach when they wanted a fat squab and built pigeon dormitories as part of their own houses: rows of nestboxes with all mod pigeon cons. In no time the pigeons were providing fresh meat, more or less on demand. Pigeons breed almost continuously right through the year, so that even in the lean months of winter there was fresh meat on the table sometimes – highly appreciated in times when most cattle and sheep were slaughtered before the winter set in, because of the shortage of feed. Pigeon houses became an important part of any grand estate, monastery or farm. With no windows and no way in for squirrels or rats, they were highly efficient, with perhaps as many as 500 pigeon holes, neatly laid out, with 500 pigeon families producing a constant supply of fat squabs. During the day, the adult birds would forage over the countryside – they didn't even have to be fed. With a fish pond, a rabbit warren, a duck decoy and a pigeon house, the lord of the manor could face winter with equanimity and a full belly. In this country nobody much bothers about squab meat nowadays because modern agricultural methods make it possible to feed cattle and sheep all winter, but shouldn't we be thinking of brushing up those old pigeon houses?

I suppose the most misunderstood and almost the least welcome wild neighbour is the bat. It is not a flying mouse, for all the flittermouse name, but belongs to a group called 'hand-wings', *Chiroptera*. They have a short thumb with a curved claw which they use as a grappling iron when climbing. Their other fingers are long and the double skin which stretches over them forms their wings. Other mammals may glide or parachute, but bats are master aviators capable of true powered flight. They roost in various places, according to species, but very often in buildings, preferring a clean and draught-free place, so you find them often enough in a fairly new, undusty and non-cobwebby house. But they are not specially faithful to one particular roosting place and may move away from time to time. Apart from hollow trees, they may choose a cave or quarry, roofs, attics or church towers for instance. Once inside, they hang themselves upside down from the roof (not much option really!) where they feel safe. The numbers in a summer breeding colony may be in the hundreds, but a few dozens are more usual. Their droppings may accumulate on the floor, but they are unobjectionable, being unsmelly, dry and anti-corrosive. On the whole I think they just improve the insulation of the house and save you a bit on your electricity bill. There might be a faint hint of truth in the old fear of bats getting in your hair, because it *could* happen, but the poor bat would be anxious to get out as quickly as possible and would certainly not be going to suck your blood. People often ask me how to destroy bats in their attics, but I try hard to persuade them to tolerate these absolutely harmless creatures which face enough problems already. Incidentally if you have your roof treated for woodworm, don't have the job done in winter when the bats will be deeply asleep; wait till May (best time for hitting woodworm beetles anyway) when they will simply make themselves scarce when you start rattling around with the spray.

Outside, and high up on your roof, is the happy sunbathing slope for pigeons and crows. And insects which emerge from the cracks and crevices around the tiles and guttering will be specially looked after by the jaunty pied wagtail. Up on the telly aerial there will on occasions be chattering starlings or swallows or maybe a singing thrush. And an itinerant woodpecker may examine the junction box for bugs, before he taps or drums his message out. There is something about telly junction boxes which pleases great spotted woodpeckers, presumably the acoustics. All these birds leave their droppings on the roof to nourish mosses and lichens, which in turn decorate the roof with oranges, greens and greys.

Roofs, chimneys, aerials and clothespoles all provide welcome song-posts for blackbirds and thrushes. Indeed, after natural perches the most popular songpost of all is a chimney pot. Herring gulls go even further and actually build their nests between chimney pots in fishing ports and seaside holiday towns – provided there is a nearby source of easy food. As a site, it is only a bizarre version of a cliff top, safe and warm. Doubtless they will extend their patronage, and maybe before very long they will be a common sight on big city roofs. They will gladly take anyone's spare crust, and as long as there is good picking on tips and perhaps some dustbins, they may soon be taking the place once filled by the scavenging red kite of Elizabethan days. At the very least they will be helping to deal with the rubbish problems of the dirtiest and most wasteful species we know – you and me!

# 5 DUSK, DARK AND DAWN

Towards evening, the pattern of activity in the garden changes. A whole work-shift of animals knocks off and prepares for bed, and the night-shift begins to stir. There may be some noisy chatter as the day birds sort themselves out for roosting. Blackbirds chuck-chuck in the hedge, a sign of tension and unease, for a whole new range of dangers is looming in the twilight. Thrushes and blackbirds will look for safety in the heart of a large bush or hedgerow. Wood pigeons go higher to the open branches of a tree. Small birds choose a variety of hidey-holes, crevices or caves in dense vegetation like ivy or behind tree bark. Towards sunset, garden parties of starlings fly off to join others in enormous flocks to perform aerial evolutions. It's a sort of rush hour in reverse, as they travel maybe thirty miles to a city centre to roost, each individual choosing his own particular spot. They think it's worth it finding it safer there and warmer. Other species, birds like rooks, finches, swallows, pigeons, flock to roost, at least outside the nesting season. Even pied wagtails, unsociable creatures most of the time, roost together; they are fond of a warm greenhouse, where their droppings may be a considerable nuisance to market gardeners.

The object is to find an undisturbed sleeping-place, somewhere to conserve energy through the cold nights. It is not easy to see solitary roosting birds, for obvious reasons. They must choose places where they are not too vulnerable to predators. Those which roost on perches have a special adaptation which ensures that they do not fall off while they are asleep: the more they relax the tighter do their toes grip the perch. A muscular locking device makes the toes curl up as the tarsal joint is flexed. In addition, they have non-slip surfaces on their feet.

Warmth is of supreme importance, and there are several techniques to achieve it. Feathers will be fluffed up to make an insulated cavity against the skin. Many species, besides man, will cuddle together through the night. Wrens are a nice example, especially when they cram their tiny bodies into a nestbox: they are sniffy about nestboxes as nesting places, but at night more than sixty individuals may squeeze into one for the benefits of group warmth. In the absence of a suitable nestbox, or a tree-hole, they may use the old nest of another hedgerow species. Usually hole-nesters like tits, sparrows and woodpeckers roost in holes of some kind. But swifts, which also use wall crevices, may actually 'roost' on the wing, flying fast asleep. In very cold weather, like wrens, they may clump together (but not on the wing!). Like swallows and swifts, house martins tend to roost late on fine evenings, when there are still plenty of insects flying about, and earlier on cold evenings.

Bees buzz home at evening time and toads are said to wait for late-comers, picking them off as they try to enter the hive. While birds and bees are off to bed, toads and reptiles and many insects are coming out to feed in the comparative safety of night. The slow worm emerges from his hidey-hole, slugs and snails make slow pilgrimages to the dining-table, worms show their faces to collect leaves off your lawn. The female glow worm, related to tropical fireflies, shows her light from a luminous organ in her tail. She climbs up a stem to show herself off and attract one of the males which will be flying about looking for the welcome sign.

Long-tailed field mouse fattening up on blackberries (*Leslie Jackman*)

Other creatures will fly to the light of your window – moths and maybugs, to be collected by late-flying swallows or fresh-flying bats. The garden cross spider will be repairing or remaking the web ready for another day's trapping. The long-tailed field mouse comes out of his burrow to search for berries, seeds and insects: specially keen on newly-sown bean and pea seeds, he will be quite content digging up bulbs in the flower border. So it is perhaps just as well that in turn there are bigger fry chasing him. Domestic cats will be on their evening patrols now and up above, in silent flight, enters the cat on wings – the superbly designed and equipped master bird and rodent-catcher, the owl.

The tawny owl is the most common garden species (barn owls prefer uninhabited buildings). Well adapted to suburban life, he has learnt to become a bird-catcher, substituting roosting blackbirds, pigeons and sparrows for his more traditional fare of rodents. Possibly Britain's most successful bird of prey, he is also a birdtable enthusiast, taking unwary songbirds as they enjoy a late meal of scraps. In fact the proportion of mammal bones in the owl's pellet is dependent on whether he is a country or garden individual: more mice and voles in the country, so more of them in the owl's diet. The suburban owl depends a great deal on small birds and is well equipped for catching them. While most birds are fast asleep, the owl makes a living under conditions which to us seem difficult. But he is designed for the job. In poor light conditions he is as much at ease as we are in daylight. He enjoys the same garden, but his is the night-shift, and he brings his senses to bear accordingly.

Most birds – hunted species – have their eyes placed on either side of the head. This allows for more-or-less all-round vision, giving maximum warning of attack. But the owl's large eyes are in the front of his facial disc and this is significant. Most predators, whether they're insect-chasing swallows or vole-chasing owls, have their eyes placed frontally so that they can see directly ahead and, using their binocular effect, judge distance. Distance is vital information to a hunter. Try closing one eye and moving your head from side to side and judge a distance. Then open both and see the improvement. Owls, perching, will bob and bow their heads about, making the most of dim light and measuring the killing swoop.

> *The Owl that, watching in the barn,*
> *Sees the mouse creeping in the corn,*
> *Sits still and shuts his round blue eyes*
> *As if he slept,—until he spies*
> *The little beast within his stretch—*
> *Then starts,—and seizes on the wretch!*
>
> 'The Barn Owl' Samuel Butler (*1612–1680*)

The owl cannot see in absolute darkness, but after all that is a rare quality in nature. Owl eyesight is much better than ours, and their hearing is exceptional, very sensitive to high-frequency sounds, such as the squeaky noises of small rodents as they scamper about the ground. Owl hearing is directional, too, with wide-spread ear 'receivers' separating stereo left-hand and right-hand sound, so that in the unlikely

event of absolute darkness they can pounce on prey using sound information alone. Nocturnal owls often hunt in broad daylight and regularly
at dusk and dawn.

Silent flight is another hunting aid for the tawny owl; floating down
on his whispering engines he surprises his victim. And of course silent
flight helps avoid confusion to the owl's listening system: he hears
mouse noises uncluttered by the sound of his own wings. They are
well-proportioned, with the weight spread over a large surface area.
He glides easily and leisurely, slow buoyant flight with a slow flap rate.
His feathers are specially modified with a velvety pile which further
damps sound (daytime owls like the little owl do not have this). Of
course nothing in life is free; that silent flight is slow and energy-
intensive, but fortunately the owl doesn't need to fly fast.

Owls have catholic tastes, and will sample anything on offer. Plenty
of night-flying moths end up as an owl's *hors d'oeuvres*. But a greater
enemy to moths is the bat, the only true flying mammal and as well
equipped in his way for insect-catching as the owl. And, like an owl, a
bat has a velvety coat, only of course his is fur instead of feather.

Bats rely mainly on sound to find their way about. Their eyes are
small, but they can see well enough: 'Blind as a bat' is yet another
unscientific and inaccurate bit of name-calling! They wake up early
enough in the evening to take full advantage of the light and the later
diurnal flying insects. Go out as dusk falls and you will usually see a
bat of some sort hawking about, putting on a sudden spurt as it homes
in on its prey. As it gets darker, cockchafers and moths are snapped up
and the real work starts.

*What hath night to do with sleep?*

'*Comus*' John Milton

The darker it gets, the more the bat relies on its superb sound
system, a sophisticated echo-location unit whereby it hears the world
instead of seeing it. Where we 'watch where we go' in avoiding obstacles, the bat 'listens where he goes' and avoids them just as effectively.
Where the obstacle is edible, say a flying moth, he just as effectively
homes in and collides with it to his advantage. He can operate at peak

efficiency in total darkness. In total blackness he knows which way is up and which way is down, for instance, and that is something no aircraft pilot would know unless he has an artificial horizon device. But man the animal is poorly equipped with sense organs, while a bat is not only designed for the job but has undergone a few million years of research and development. He has first-class instrumentation. His ears are very sensitive. The middle ear is concerned with sounds, with echo-location, but the inner ear is concerned with orientation and altitude. The labyrinth, part of the inner ear concerned with balance, is designed to feed information about movements and accelerations of the head in relation to the rest of the body. Bats are small, the information results in instructions which reach the appropriate muscles quickly and any tendency to roll or pitch or yaw or stall is quickly counteracted. The situation is much the same with birds, and indeed with creatures like flies, but even simple organisms like jellyfish which have no eyes worth talking about maintain a stable posture in the sea, because they are specially adapted for the job.

Bats are entirely useful beasts to welcome to your garden. They eat nothing but insects. Perhaps their spooky and jittery flight is unattractive, and of course they are creatures of the night: the result is that people are prejudiced and ignorant about them, and so, like the owl, they represent fear and foreboding.

There is nothing sinister about the hedgehog, with his carefree shuffling and scrunching around the shrubbery and borders. Everyone's favourite, he is the most welcome wild inhabitant of a garden. He eats mainly insects, insect larvae and worms. No bad habits, no trouble, easy to identify, prickly by coat but not by character, he is abundant in suburban areas, especially around old houses and unkept gardens. Garden life suits him, food prospects are good and predators few.

Along with the mole and the shrews he is a representative of the *Insectivora*, an order of animals which feeds mainly on insects. So he is not a fast-mover, and although he has good teeth he doesn't make a great deal of use of them in defence. Faced with an attacker, he simply curls up to hide his face and his soft underbelly and erects his sharp spines as a prickly and impenetrable barrier. And a very effective defence it must be, to judge from the nonchalant way the animal

Hunting hedgehog (*Stephen Dalton*)

chunters its way round the leafy borders of the garden. But this technique comes sadly adrift when, as so often happens, he is discovered in the roadway by the headlights of a car. Rolling up, instead of running off, he risks a flattening.

A hedgehog is a noisy hunter, snuffling and grunting, sniffing and scenting with a disregard for peace and quiet, yet with very sensitive moist nose-membranes, which smell out the food possibilities. He turns over leaves and mosses, grubbing about. A loud and vulgar snort may greet the discovery of a toothsome morsel like a snail. And then, as you would by now expect, he proceeds to eat it on the spot with noisy enjoyment, snap, crackle and pop. Woodlice, slugs and worms, scraps from the birdtable, he relishes them all. But he needs a big garden to sustain him, or he will climb walls like a born mountaineer and forage next door as well. Many people cherish him, putting out dishes of minced meat and egg, milk and cheese; he never seems wild about minced meat, his plebeian taste is well pleased with a slice of factory bread and a piece of fruit cake! If you frighten him by appearing suddenly he will jump sideways and erect his spines, possibly

Hedgehogs circling in courtship ritual

curling up, but as often as not he will ignore you in a lordly manner and allow you to join him in the hunt.

Over a period you will find it easy to tame him. Slow but sure is the rule. Don't stare him in the face, move quietly but freely. Feed him regularly, and if you can afford mealworms (and the robin doesn't demand them all) that will accelerate the process.

On midsummer nights on the open lawn you may see the bucolic courtship of the hedgehogs, where one partner circles round and round the other for what seems like hours. The nest will be made against tree roots, in a compost heap or woodpile or in brambles. It is made of grass and leaves, in the form of a mound. Then the hog burrows into it and shapes a hollow chamber. It is not easy to find, and sadly is too often the victim of an accident with a garden fork. The young hedge-hogs are born blind, their spines are soft and white but soon superseded by the familiar dark ones which harden slowly over a period of weeks. The first litter may be born in May or June, leaving the nest in July, but there is often a second, and it is in late summer that you are most likely to see the young out of the nest. Life may be very tough on the later juveniles, as they have little time to build up fat reserves to help them survive the winter. But there is no more charming sight than an adult hedgehog leading a caravan of young ones about the garden as they learn the trade.

Larger mammals are not so universally welcome in the garden. Deer fawns may have spawned the bambi legend, but your real-life flesh-and-blood roe deer will create havoc. Foxes have the sense to cause minimal local disturbance apart from a tendency to untidiness, but a badger in the garden is a mixed blessing, however well disposed you might be. The few people I have known who have had badgers on their garden checklist have just had to give in gracefully and give up all thoughts of gardening in the conventional sense. The sett is usually, but not invariably, on sloping ground, in hilly country or woodland edge, so if your garden isn't, you can relax. But the wood doesn't have to be a big one, and access to a golf course, railway embankment, park or gravel pit may be positive assets for a badger. There will need to be water of some sort nearby, preferably a stream or river. If all the signs are propitious, then the excavating and earthworks begin, and you are going to have an uncomfortable garden-guest. The entrance holes are large, and there may be a lot of them. There will be well-trodden paths and play places, and few obstructions will be tolerated. There won't be much mess about, certainly not waste food, but possibly some stray bedding material like bracken and grasses. Over a period of years the whole character of your property will be changed. The landscaping will be on the grand scale, with much displacement of soil by the time Capability Badger has finished work.

The lawn will be explored for earthworms with many scratchings and scrapings, and at a discreet distance from the sett there will be dung pits, small shallow diggings decorated with the badger's offerings. A very fastidious animal.

In the country badgers are common partly because they have the good sense to keep a low profile. Centuries of persecution and abuse have taught them to keep themselves to themselves in the interests of survival. Plenty of farmers have badger setts under their chicken houses, and no one is any the worse off. Sometimes people don't ever know they're there, but in your garden you cannot fail to know about it.

But having said all the bad things you don't have to look far for the good ones. No trouble during the day, the badger will come out at dusk and put on a display of great appeal. It is a beautiful animal to see, big and woolly. It has an endearing habit of scratching with gay abandon, has playful cubs, and if you put out food, it will come right up to the window to feed by your side. Worms and beetles may be its natural diet, but it will accept chocolate or honey with enthusiasm. Have some regard for its teeth, though, for chocolate can't be too good for it; perhaps minced meat and scraps would be more thoughtful. It will be regular in its habits and will prefer you to be the same. From its point of view you are an acceptable neighbour and provided you keep yourself to yourself it will repay the compliment. It is unlikely to eat the cat, or your bantams, but it might enjoy your beans, so lay a rope soaked in diesel oil around them, for badgers don't like its smell.

Why do they have that striking white head, with the two bold black stripes down through the eye? Ernest Neal thinks it is not a disruptive pattern, nothing to do with matching moonlight shafts of light between dark trees. He thinks it is a warning device. Like the diagonal stripes on heavy lorries it means 'I am dangerous, get out of the way'. Badgers,

Badger on its regular visit to the scrap plate; the hedgehog in the background has to wait its turn (*Pat Morris*)

like hedgehogs, hardly bother to avoid drawing attention to themselves; they blunder through the undergrowth like bulldozers. Hedgehogs feel safe underneath all those prickles; maybe badgers feel safe just because they're big and strong, with powerful teeth. They've no need to bother about their prey hearing them coming; most of their prey species wouldn't know what was happening till it was too late, and are too slow to escape anyway. The badger is a forager by nature, very different in character and interests from that other garden beast, the fox.

Foxes are not uncommon garden residents. Many people don't even know they're there. Many more people know they're there and take pleasure in the knowledge, for the fox is one of those animals for which we have a fellow-feeling. It is always a significant sign when we give an animal a nickname and perhaps we like the somewhat disreputable, cunning nature of the beast. Like us, or rather like something we used to be, reynard or old daddy fox is a hunter and an opportunist. He takes risks and cocks a snook when the occasion demands it. He is a carnivore and particularly intelligent, with a large brain for his size. He has acute senses, he is fast and cheeky. For all the nonsense written in newspapers whenever there's a hard winter, he is not a pack animal and there is no chance that he will terrorise the neighbourhood. Perhaps this sort of legend stems from a dim memory of the wolf packs which scourged wild country a long time ago (the wolf persisted in Scotland until the eighteenth century).

Anyway, the fox does well in the suburbs, mostly because people like to see him. He will eat anything, scavenging birdtables and litter bins, compost heaps and dustbins. Very often the noise of the dustbin lid being upturned is the first sign that he is about, and many people have had their first view of a fox from the bedroom window. In the days not so long ago when offal was chucked into the streets, our towns were scavenged by crows and black kites; today's scavengers are pigeons, herring gulls and foxes.

Foxes take pigeons and poultry when they get the chance. Many an exotic duck or goose from an ornamental pond ends up feeding a fox family under the garden shed. They have been known to dash out and take food from delivery vans. Possibly they nobble an occasional domestic cat, but there is more talk than evidence.

107

Fox about town (*Joe B. Blossom*)

Foxes commonly set up their home earth under a shed at the bottom of the garden, knowing they're on to a good thing: no tiresome disturbance from the Hunt, a ready supply of food and a quiet place to spend the day before coming out at dusk to be watched from the window by the fellow who kindly puts out a tray of food or makes sure the birdtable is well stocked. He will quickly learn to put in a regular appearance. His bad habits are easily defined and not too awful to be tolerated. He has a powerful smell, and the vicinity of the earth is well-marked and he has an untidy tendency to strew old bones and chicken feathers about. All he asks in return is peace and quiet for his daytime sleep in a well-drained and dry place. It doesn't have to be underground – a hole in the wall or a treetrunk will do. If all goes well, he will eventually invite a vixen to shack up with him and there will be a half-a-dozen foxcubs. Then the vixen will stay away all day, but return at dusk with food. She yaps, and out come the cubs to feed and then to play. Foxes and dogs may chase each other happily round and round a house without any malice aforethought. They even play with cats. For the cubs, of course, playing is a serious affair. Typical behaviour for carnivores, it is the process of learning to hunt and kill, just as the playful kitten learns to smell and pounce, explores the lie of the land and discovers how to stalk. Theirs is very much the world of the cat, rather than the typical puppy play which mostly involves headlong chase, rip and tear.

Foxes have been seen playing in the Royal Wimbledon Golf Club's sandy bunkers. They even run off with golf balls, later found severely chewed! And they are well established in city parks. Some years ago a philistine town council had the nerve to invite a Hunt to a local park, after geese and ducks had been killed in the nearby zoo. But the zoo was the intruder, having usurped some of the semi-wild acreage from its rightful owners, the wild animals including foxes.

Headlight fox hunts through city centres have been organised – with the object of counting them, not killing them, I hasten to add. In Bristol, 14 foxes were counted between 4.00 and 6.00 am; in suburban Plymouth, starting at 3.30 one morning and hunting with 15 cars and 40 observers over a total of 450 miles, all in residential areas, we saw 7 foxes, 14 cats, 12 rabbits, 2 dogs, 2 rats, 2 mice, 1 vole, 1 bat and 5 tawny owls. Two days before the count a fox had been seen in broad

Fox cubs at play

Badger with cubs

daylight. The technique is not really very satisfactory as lots of animals
must be missed, but a load of fun.

Rabbits are rarely welcome in a garden, although they make good
lawnmowers at first. If they are about you'll see them at dusk and at
dawn, nibbling away in that delicate manner. But put some netting
around your young trees, for they won't withstand the onslaught of
those bark and bud nibblers. As a landscape artist the rabbit is second
only to the badger, and for that reason alone can be an uncomfortable
neighbour. The extensive burrowings erode banks and boundaries, and
their feeding degrades the lawn to an ever more closely nibbled sward
that ends up as a moss patch broken only by clumps of ragwort.

> *The rabbit has a charming face;*
> *Its private life is a disgrace.*
> *I really dare not name to you*
> *The awful things that rabbits do.*

Anon

Dawn is a good time to do your garden-watching. The nocturnal animals are still finishing their night's work and now is your best chance to see foxes, badgers, rabbits and hedgehogs before they retire. And now is the time for diurnal birds to wake up and sing to proclaim a new day. There are fewer people about, and less human disturbance means more wildlife to be seen. The early risers are up for the worms and the slug-a-beds are late risers for perfectly good reasons: until the warmth of the sun starts some air-rising thermals going there's not much action from flying insects. So swallows and swifts and martins stay in bed. But soon enough the new shift takes over and a whole new hunting day begins.

*Come into the garden, Maud,*
*For the black bat, night, has flown.*

'*Maud*' Tennyson

# 6 HARD TIMES, SLEEPY TIMES

Your lawn and birdtable will be crowded in July and August, when the season's crop of young birds is bursting on to the scene, but quite suddenly you may find that all is quiet in September. The parties of noisy blue tits vanish. Nothing has gone wrong. They have simply deserted you temporarily while the feeding is better elsewhere. For this is the time when wild fruits, seeds and nuts are plentiful in the fields, woods and hedgerows. Be pleased for them while they enjoy the harvest, and be patient because in a month or two they will be trickling back to the garden with fat reserves well stocked and ready to face the winter.

Winter is a testing time, and the inevitable process of natural selection will ensure that a proportion of every family will die, for die they must if a long-term stable population is to be maintained. It is easy to talk in high-flown general terms, but for each and every individual the test is entirely personal and every last individual is reluctant to be the one that goes under. There are four alternatives open to him. In the face of approaching food shortage he can stuff himself and sleep it out in hibernation, he can migrate to a more sympathetic climate, he can stay put and forage harder, or he can die.

Approaching winter means a shorter hunting day and it means a falling temperature requiring more energy to keep warm. Most plants reduce their growth rate, providing little food, so a late-developer like ivy is doubly welcome. Blooming in November, its inconspicuous flower clusters provide a last fling for nectar-hungry insects. Wasps and flies feast on it, picking up pollen and distributing it, laying the foundation for the fruiting which in its turn will be much appreciated by birds in the depth of winter. Sadly, that fruiting will not be seen by a lot of the insects which swarm about the flowers.

Most insects inevitably die at the first real onset of winter as the lack of nectar begins to be felt, but they leave behind eggs or pupae which will endure until the warmth of spring. Not all insects die; a small proportion will find a sympathetic hidey-hole in a crevice or buried in leaf litter, there to sit tight and hope to avoid the hunting birds. Mosquitoes will choose an outhouse or cellar, coming out on warm winter days for a quick sustaining meal of your blood. In many cases it is the female of an insect species which faces winter while all the males have died. The female earwig sleeps through the hard months, depositing her eggs in a soil burrow, caring for them when they hatch until they are old enough to fend for themselves; an unusual procedure for insects. Ladybirds sit out the aphidless months by hibernating amongst the grassy roots of the lawn, or by gathering in masses behind loose bark or in the corner of a window frame. Tortoise-shell and peacock butterflies shelter in ivy or in garden sheds, or spend the winter in a fold of your curtains or clinging to the brick-work. But most die. In the beehive when the outside temperature drops the workers cluster together maintaining a core temperature of 20°C. The ones on the outside die, the lucky ones in the middle survive to new life in the spring. The garden snail makes his way to ancestral halls in stone walls and under stones in the rockery, joining with his mates and closing his shell with a mucus seal to keep out the cold.

So winter only needs to show its face for the insects to begin to disappear, facing the birds which depend on them with the choice of migrating or sticking it out. For any species which depends largely on flying insects, it is migrate or die. And in migrating they are playing a part in a pattern which holds good all over the world. Blue whales spend the winter season in temperate zones, then journey to the polar icecaps for the summer period of abundant plankton. Many fish travel great distances to enjoy the best plankton seasons. On the African plains great herds of ungulates travel hundreds of miles to make best use of seasonal grass.

The process comes right into our gardens when the swallows and house martins begin to congregate on clothes lines and telegraph wires. Over a period of many days they group together in ever larger numbers waiting for the signal, a combination of decreasing insect availability, falling temperature and shorter days. For the departure day, they choose settled weather and clear skies if they get the chance. The most spectacular visible migration will occur when the weather clears after a bad patch. They fly off with well-stocked bodies and a thick layer of

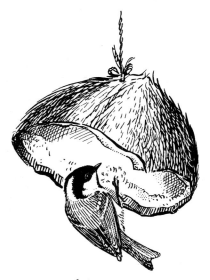

Coal tit at coconut

fat under the skin, fuel reserves which will carry them all the way to Africa. Those swallows which survive the journey will find themselves perhaps in the suburbs of Johannesburg. I have been in one of the city's parks on a January evening when the sky was dark with countless thousands of 'our' swallows dropping in to roost in the reedbeds of a lake.

> *The swallow, privileged above the rest*
> *Of all the birds as man's familiar guest,*
> *Pursues the sun in summer, brisk and bold,*
> *But wisely shuns the persecuting cold.*

'*The Swallow*' John Dryden (*1631–1700*)

Many swallows and house martins run things very close in leaving this country. A house martin may successfully rear three broods of chicks, and then it will be well into November, even December, before they are ready to migrate. Inevitably a higher percentage of these late starters will come to grief in crossing the Alps. A very few will not risk it, and stay behind to overwinter; but it must be a mild winter for them to have any chance of survival.

Those species which elect to stick it out in Britain for the winter face a tough time. It is not so much the cold weather that is the problem – given a decent reserve of fat they can stay warm, even roosting with snow on their plumage. The problem is getting enough to eat. Snails are hidden, insects are deep in crevices or lost in leaf litter. Foraging is a serious business; there is little time for singing about the coming season of courtship. Only the fiercely territorial robin summons up enough energy to entertain us with his thin song. The hedges and gardens ring with the more utilitarian calls of chaffinch and long-tailed tit parties as they keep in touch with each other.

> *The north wind doth blow,*
> *And we shall have snow,*
> *And what will the robin do then?*
> > *Poor thing.*

'*Songs for the Nursery*' (*1805*)

Waxwings feeding on berries

As if life wasn't already hard enough in winter, the resident birds are joined by large numbers of foreigners who have migrated to us rather than away from us. Fleeing from the icy winter wastes of Scandinavia, fieldfares and redwings come in their thousands, to compete for the hawthorn and holly berries and for the rotting windfall fruit. In really

116

bad weather a well-stocked bird feeding station will undoubtedly help many to survive.

Fieldfares and redwings, those Scandinavian thrushes, join us regularly each winter, but at odd intervals there may be an invasion of a species which is so remarkably coloured that we think they have escaped from an aviary. Waxwings have a black tail with a yellow tip, chestnut body and striking chestnut crest. Strangest of all, they have scarlet waxy tips to their secondary wing feathers. They are not easily missed, as they work along the hedgerows looking for rowan, hawthorn and ivy berries. They may invade a garden to search for *Berberis* and *Cotoneaster* berries, or for the remains of apples and pears. Waxwings probably only appear in this country when the autumn food crop fails in Eastern Europe. Usually they show up first in Yorkshire and Norfolk in mid October, but then find their way down to Kent, then westwards sometimes as far as Ireland in November. Noticeably tame, once having arrived they may stay as late as April.

Berries of one kind and another are a staple midwinter diet; ivy berries are in demand by blackbirds and thrushes. But in midwinter those roving flocks of rooks and starlings will be hard at work quartering lawns and digging in the search for leatherjackets, beetles and molluscs. One of the most effective ways of beating the problem of winter is to be an opportunist feeder, taking advantage of anything that is on offer, and that is one of the mainstays of the starling success. His flexibility allows him to survive difficult periods.

Fruit, berries and birdtable food are all much in demand, but many animals are searching most of all for seeds. An oak tree may shed as many as 90,000 acorns every year; most go to feed the birds or groundfeeders like mice, who nibble both seeds and shoots. The long-tailed field mouse will bury them as a foodstore in a separate chamber attached to his underground nest.

But jays are the master acorn-dealers. In winter acorns form a staple diet, and an astonishing number are stored hidden in the ground or in odd nooks and crannies, often some way from the tree. And it is not a random process. Once buried, the jay knows exactly where to find them. He holds the nut with his feet, bites off the shell and then eats it piece by piece at leisure.

Acorns and hazel nuts are good news for many other species, nut-hatches and rooks for instance, and for squirrels, which also hoard them in stores. Given the opportunity, many tits will hide peanuts or beech mast for a rainy day. Willow tits wedge nuts in fence posts and in the joints of rustic trellis work. Coal tits have hidden them in clumps of grass, even brussels sprout tops, or in the soil.

So food stores help many animals to tide themselves over a rough patch of winter. Especially is this true of both red and grey squirrels. Neither of them hibernate, and winter is the time they are most often seen doing their birdtable acrobatics. Not so many animals hibernate as people think, especially in this country. Many of them, having fed and fattened themselves in autumn, just slow down their activity for the winter, with a consequently reduced demand on their energy resources.

Grass snakes and slow worms find a convenient hole in a bank or a cavity amongst tree roots in October and stay there till March. Newts find a hole in the ground or under a stone or log, or in a cellar, return-

Acorns are the staple diet for jays in winter (*Jane Burton*)

Badger in bracken

ing to the breeding pond in February or March. Frogs hibernate in or near the pond, buried in soft mud or in bank holes, but not always in the water. In areas tending to have mild winters, they hardly bother to hibernate at all and can be seen soon after Christmas in garden ponds.

Most British mammals do the same. While some, like the squirrels, store food and don't even consider hibernation, many of the others slow down the pace of life a little. The fox remains active, so does the badger, though he spends more time below ground. Only the hedgehog and the bat really hibernate. The hedgehog accumulates as much fat as he can in the autumn. But then chemical changes take place in his body; the sugars in his blood decrease. When the ground temperature hits somewhere around 16°C it triggers the mechanism and he sinks into a winter sleep, but it is not deep until the temperature is somewhere about 9°C. The lower the autumn temperatures, the sooner he goes into hibernation, but often he remains active well into December before he disappears into his winter nest of insulating leaves, probably in a hedge-bottom hole or amongst tree roots.

Hibernating greater horseshoe bats (*Eric Hosking*)

During hibernation the hedgehog metabolism is slower, his body heat dropping from about 35°C to less than 10°C, using less of his fat reserves, his heartbeat and respiration are slowed, and to all intents and purposes he becomes a near cold-blooded animal. But in spite of general belief he does not spend the winter inactive; every now and then he will wake up and emerge to forage and refill his fuel tanks of fat.

Bats are the only mammals equipped for migration by flight, but they opt out of the rigours of winter by going to sleep. As with the hedgehog, it is only a partial hibernation and you will often see them hunting on a mild sunny evening or morning; but there are not enough flying insects about to sustain them at full activity. They face the winter by building up a thick layer of fat under the skin, and then congregating in large numbers in their winter caves or lofts, hanging upside down from the roof, shrouded in their skin wings, using only a hundredth of the oxygen they normally breathe.

The gradually lengthening days and the gentle warmth of spring wake the sleepers and hearten the survivors of the tough brigade which struggle on against all the odds. The winter visitors take off to the insect-rich hunting grounds of the arctic and Siberian wastes and the returning migrants rejoin us for the breeding season, ready to share in the search for awakening and multiplying insects. The cycle repeats itself, again and again, allowing only minor variations and extremely slow changes to the grand theme. Long may it continue.

# BOOKS AND SOCIETIES

**BIRDS**
>For identification: *A Field Guide to the Birds of Britain and Europe* Peterson, Mountfort and Hollom (Collins)
>For further information: *The Popular Handbook of British Birds* P. A. D. Hollom (Witherby)
>Birdtables, nestboxes. *The New Bird Table Book* Tony Soper (David & Charles)

**MAMMALS**
>*The Handbook of British Mammals* H. N. Southern (Blackwell)
>*British Mammals* L. Harrison Matthews (Collins)

**INSECTS**
>*The Oxford Book of Insects* John Burton (Oxford)
>*A Field Guide to the Insects of Britain* Michael Chinery (Collins)
>*Insect Natural History* A. D. Imms (Collins)
>*Pleasure from Insects* Michael Tweedie (David & Charles)

**SPIDERS**
>*The World of Spiders* W. S. Bristowe (Collins)

**REPTILES AND AMPHIBIANS**
>*The British Reptiles and Amphibians* Malcolm Smith (Collins)
>*The Tailed Amphibians of Europe* J. W. Steward (David & Charles)

**SOIL**
>*The World of Soil* Sir E. John Russell (Collins)

FUNGI

> *Mushrooms and Toadstools* John Ramsbottom (Collins)
> *Mushrooms and other Fungi* Augusto Rinaldi and Vassili Tyndalo
> (Hamlyn)

The *Wayside and Woodland* series published by Warne is good value, and for an inexpensive guide any volume in the natural history series of Hamlyn all-colour paperbacks is unbeatable.

ALL GARDEN NATURALISTS should support the Royal Society for the Protection of Birds (brochure from RSPB, Sandy, Bedfordshire). In spite of its name, the Society is deeply concerned with the management of land and resources in a way which allows breathing space for all living creatures. Joining it is one of the most powerful and effective ways of demonstrating that you care for wildlife. First class journal and access to many nature reserves. Lively junior section is the Young Ornithologists Club. If you develop a more academic interest in birds, join the British Trust for Ornithology (brochure from BTO, Beech Grove, Tring, Herts.).

*British Birds* is the magazine for birdwatchers. Monthly, published by Blackwell.

*Wildlife* is a general interest natural history magazine, with worldwide coverage. Published monthly by Nigel Sitwell, 243 Kings Road, London SW3 5EA.

# SCIENTIFIC NAMES

(Hedge sparrow to some, dunnock to others, but *Prunella modularis* all over the world! The value of scientific names is that, being based on a dead language – Latin – they are not subject to changes brought about by time and common usage).

Ant, black garden   *Lasius niger*
Badger   *Meles meles*
Bat, greater horseshoe   *Rhinolophus ferrumequinum*
Bee, bumble   genus *Bombus*
    honey   *Apis mellifera*
    leafcutter   *Megachile centuncularis*
    mining   *Andrena arnata*
Beetle, carrion   *Thanatophilus sp.*
    sexton   *Necrophorus sp.*
Blackbird   *Turdus merula*
Blackcap   *Sylvia atricapilla*
Blackfly superfamily   *APHIDOIDEA*
Butterfly, cabbage white   *Pieris brassicae*
Buzzard   *Buteo buteo*
Cat   *Felis domesticus*
Chaffinch   *Fringilla coelebs*
Chiffchaff   *Phylloscopus collybita*
Cockchafer   *Melolontha melolontha*
Crow, carrion   *Corvus corone*
Cuckoo   *Cuculus canorus*
Dunnock   *Prunella modularis*
Fieldfare   *Turdus pilaris*
Fox   *Vulpes vulpes*

Frog, common   *Rana temporaria*
Froghopper   *Philaenus spumarius*
Goldfinch   *Carduelis carduelis*
Greenfinch   *Carduelis chloris*
Greenfly   superfamily *APHIDOIDEA*
Gull, herring   *Larus argentatus*
Hedgehog   *Erinaceus europaeus*
Hoopoe   *Upapa epops*
Jackdaw   *Corvus monedula*
Jay   *Garrulus glandarius*
Kestrel   *Falco tinnunculus*
Ladybird   family *COCCINELIDAE*
Leatherjacket   *Tipula paludosa*
Magpie   *Pica pica*
Martin, house   *Delichon urbica*
Maybug   *Melolontha melolontha*
Mole   *Talpa europaea*
Mosquito   family *CULICIDAE*
Mouse, house   *Mus musculus*
     long-tailed field   *Apodemus sylvaticus*
Mushroom, fairy ring   *Marasmius oreades*
     field   *Psalliota campestris*
Newt, common   *Triturus vulgaris*
Nuthatch   *Sitta europaea*
Owl, barn   *Tyto alba*
     little   *Athene noctua*
     tawny   *Strix aluco*
Pipit, meadow   *Anthus pratensis*
Rabbit   *Oryctolagus cuniculus*
Redwing   *Turdus iliacus*
Robin   *Erithacus rubecula*
Rock dove   *Columba livia*
Shrew, common   *Sorex araneus*
Skylark   *Alauda arvensis*
Slow worm   *Anguis fragilis*
Slug, garden   *Arion hortensis*

great grey   *Limax maximus*
netted   *Agriolimax reticulatus*
Snail, banded   *Cepaea sp.*
common   *Helix aspersa*
roman   *Helix pomatia*
Snake, grass   *Natrix natrix*
Snipe   *Gallinago gallinago*
Sparrow, hedge   *Prunella modularis*
house   *Passer domesticus*
Sparrowhawk   *Accipiter nisus*
Spider, garden cross   *Araneus diadematus*
Squirrel, grey   *Sciurus carolinensis*
red   *Sciurus vulgaris*
Starling   *Sturnus vulgaris*
Stickleback   *Gasterosteus aculeatus*
Stone curlew   *Burhinus oedicnemu*
Swallow   *Hirundo rustica*
Swift   *Apus apus*
Thrush, mistle   *Turdus viscivorus*
song   *Turdus philomelos*
Tit, bearded   *Panurus biarmicus*
blue   *Parus caeruleus*
great   *Parus major*
long-tailed   *Aegithalos caudatus*
Toad, common   *Bufo bufo*
Treecreeper   *Certhia familiaris*
Wagtail, pied   *Motacilla alba*
Warbler, dartford   *Sylvia undata*
Wasp, common   *Vespula vulgaris*
Waxwing   *Bombycilla garrulus*
Wheatear   *Oenanthe oenanthe*
Woodpecker, great spotted   *Dendrocopos major*
green   *Pica viridis*
Wood pigeon   *Columba palumbus*
Worm, earth   *Lumbricus terrestris*
Wren   *Troglodytes troglodytes*

# INDEX